FEMINIST, QUEER, ANTICOLONIAL PROPOSITIONS FOR HACKING THE ANTHROPOCENE: ARCHIVE

Edited By

Jennifer Mae Hamilton

Susan Reid

Pia van Gelder

Astrida Neimanis

()

OPEN HUMANITIES PRESS

London 2021

First edition published by Open Humanities Press 2021
Copyright © the authors 2021

Freely available online at:
http://www.openhumanitiespress.org/books/titles/feminist-queer-anticolonial-propositions-for-hacking-the-anthropocene/

Cover image: Pussy Print by Betty Grumble, done with eco gentle paints and with respect to all embodied printers and players before, alongside and ahead.

Type Design Jo Stirling.
Typeset using Fira Sans and Tinos.

Print ISBN: 978-1-78542-067-2
PDF ISBN: 978-1-78542-066-5
ePub ISBN: 978-1-78542-068-9

( )

OPEN HUMANITIES PRESS

Open Humanities Press is an international, scholar-led, open access publishing collective whose mission is to make leading works of contemporary critical thought freely available worldwide.

More at http://openhumanitiespress.org

For many non-scientists, the images and language of climate change and accompanying ecological events present as enigmatic signs. They elicit profound anxieties even as they conjure new ways of seeing the world. Environmental events are thus pushing up to the surface what are fundamentally literary problematics of writing and reading. OHP's Seed Books address the impact of today's new climate imaginaries. In fluid, permeable books funded by Sweden's The Seed Box: A Mistra-Formas Environmental Humanities Collaboratory, we are exploring how today's new visual and cognitive landscapes are engendering new collaborative textual practices in Humanities disciplines.

Read more at https://theseedbox.se/

Contents

Part 3: Hacking the Anthropocene 3: Want (2018)

An Archive of an Epoch that Almost Was

Astrida Neimanis

What was the Anthropocene?

Oops, you just missed it. After a decade of enthusiasm, Anthropocenomania is finally waning. Less than any scientific disagreement with the term, this fall from favour reflects critiques of the Anthropocene imaginary: *Since when have (certain) humans not been destroying (certain) kinds of life on earth? Who does this imaginary make expendable, and what kinds of relations does it reify?* When Donna Haraway suggested that our job was "to make the Anthropocene as short/thin as possible" (Haraway 2015), it seems many were already helping the cause. The assumptions and exclusions that undergirded this imaginary have been called out.

We could simply say: *Donna, we did it!* But things are rarely that simple. Afterall, many communities have been involved in this counterlabour of "doing it" since long before the Anthropocene was a twinkle in any chronostratigrapher's eye. And just as significantly, the conditions of possibility for imagining an "Age of Man" have hardly gone away. Addressing the assumptions and omissions of this Epoch That Almost Was (even and especially if in some ways *it still is*) thus requires archaeological work.

This introduction thus rehearses a specific-if-tentacular feminist endeavor begun in Sydney, Australia in 2015, that sought to tell the story of the Anthropocene otherwise. Even if challenging the Anthropocene discourse seems less urgent now, as feminists we know the value of studying our own histories, examining our tactics, and chronicling our labours (Hamilton and Neimanis, 2018). This is how we move forward and how we endure.

A New Geological Epoch?

In a binding vote released on 21 May 2019, the Anthropocene Working Group (AWG) proposed recognition of the Anthropocene as a formal chorono-stratigraphic unit. This work, initiated in the early years of the new millennium, supports the AWG's position that "we humans" are profoundly altering Holocenic plantetary systems in consequential ways.

For some, such pronouncements were nothing more than a rallying confirmation of US against IT. In this updated iteration of the "Man versus Nature" binary, Nature as canvas upon which Man paints his culture was transformed into the whole earth as a medium that the genius human could master and mould. If the planet was in trouble, surely we could engineer ourselves out of it: only a "Good Anthropocene" would save us now!

Forgive us for being sceptical of such approaches. If the Anthropocene could ironically be read as the material mark of a human exceptionalist approach to life, why would we mend our ways with a concept that put an uncritical and undifferentiated version of the human right back at the centre? This scepticism, however, would do little to curb the mess that we humans were (still) making. It remains no simple task, after all, to undo the material transformations that constitute this supposed new epoch. Even more challenging (but not impossible!) is dismantling colonial, capitalist, heteropatriachal systems that fossil-fuel these violences.

Luckily then, for others the pronouncement of the Anthropocene also offered an opportunity for reflection. Some humans were sobered by these ideas, even if their discursive premises were flawed. In imagining ourselves as an active species within a responsive context, the externalities of our own species-being finally got really real.

So a wholesale *rejection* of the Anthropocene was not the ticket. Instead, we sought tactics that might more modestly, but no less transformatively, interrupt the practices and assumptions that shored up the Anthropocene discourse. For instance, as feminist, queer, antiracist and anticolonial makers and thinkers insist, while humans may all be in this together, we are in it in very different ways. Our humanness is textured by compelling differences in circumstance, location, and accountability. "We" build the Anthropocene differently, and "we" bear its burdens and reap its rewards differently, too. And, as Kathryn Yusoff (2018), among others, have argued, some of "us" have been living in the shadow of the Anthropocene for centuries; the "human" impact on planetary systems co-emerges with colonialism and imperialism, which have been violently interrupting and ending lifeworlds long before any proposed "new" epoch.

Part of our counterproposition to the Anthropocene discourse, then, was to insist on the urgent insights that the difference of such perspectives could offer. After all, feminist, Indigenous, queer and anti-racist activists and scholars, among others, have long been at the vanguard of critical approaches to matters concerning the question of "the human" (for example, see Wynter [McKittrick, Ed., 2015] and Jackson, 2020). Who better, then, to offer expertise on the implications of this new human-forged age? The Anthropocene both "re-performs this spatial disloca- tion of 'others' (once again alienating marginalized people from writing their own histories)" while also "naturalising the 'we' of Western culture" (Yusoff, 2015). Against this push of dislocation, we wanted to insist that *you* (whoever you are) *belong here*. How could this belonging be taken up, made accountable, and become a small but vital act of transformation?

And, while in dialogue with scientists and policy makers, this archive champions the contributions of artists, poets, essayists, scholars. If the stakes of the Anthropocene were (and remain) not only geological and biological, but profoundly social and cultural, then the voices of those most attuned to such mat- ters are crucial. We wanted to know, for example: how can art- making and creative engagement with non-human worlds invite us to contemplate different strategies for getting on with our worldly companions, in all of their diversity? How might fiction spur us to imagine decolonial and multispecies futures in new ways? How can practitioners of sociology, design, gender stud- ies, philosophy, anthropology, archeology, literary studies, his- tory, and more, all offer insights into the paradoxical premises of the Anthropocene? We sought to make different kinds of conver- sations possible.

In short, the Anthropocene was not a problem to be solved, but both a practice and a concept to be hacked.

Don't Reject It, Just Hack It

- Hacking (1) / to deploy unauthorised actants to interrupt, to intervene, to use the system against itself. To torque the method in order to produce results that serve different bodies, and different purposes. To put a spanner in the works. As in: hacking the mainframe, hacking into the database. As in: I've been hacked!

- Hacking (2) / to withstand, to bear, to carry the burden. As in: can you hack it? Or: I just can't hack it. As in: try to hack it just a little longer.

- Hacking (3) / to cut into, to chop, perhaps recklessly, or determinedly. To channel anger and rage. Potentially violent and destructive. Potentially cathartic. In reference to one's work or project: to radically subtract, clarify, and determine what is excessive or optional, and what, conversely, cannot be done without.

- Hacking (4) / to cough wretchedly. To attempt to rid oneself of disturbing bits of matter. As in: I feel like I'm hacking up a lung. As in: a hacking cough, which may be a persistent endeavour without the satisfaction of immediate relief.

The key question that this collection thus poses is: What might it mean to hack the Anthropocene, as a collaborative and experimental endeavour? How might "hacking" – in any or all of these various inflections – offer transformative tactics for approaching the Age of Man? While one approach might be to stealthily infect the Anthropocene system with an Otherwise, another might be to seek ways of building better worlds in the inevitable ruins of our (or others') making, and with whatever grace we can muster. Hacking the Anthropocene might ask us to divest ourselves of the unnecessary conceits of capitalist consumerism that is

Astrida Neimanis

surely one of its prime engines – to hack away at the excessive excess (while always leaving room for the essential excess). Or it might be just a metaphorical clearing of our airways. We may just need a little breathing room. This collection chronicles variations on all of these efforts.

Our objective in hacking the Anthropocene was thus not to simply reject it, but rather to invite a counterproposition: how can the proposition of the International Stratigraphic Commission be reimagined, repurposed, reoriented?

Tactics for Hacking

Hacking—both this collection and the events that gave rise to it— proposes that the tools and resources for thinking and making an alternative future already exist in the scholarship and activism of those historically excluded from the hegemony named by the Anthropocene. Just as many have had to hack (read: endure) the persistence of a dominant white, colonial, masculinist, heteronormative modernity, so too have we hacked (read: torqued and reprogrammed) into it via protest, critique, deconstructive analysis, community building, creative production, and policy making. We suggest that the ecological challenges we face are better served when addressed not as an issue discrete from extant human challenges, but taken as another dimension in an ongoing tradition of inclusive feminist critiques of power, violence, and injustice.

Archiving—despite its conservative connotations of preservation and status quo—is also a hacking tactic. Long participating in counter-hegemonic projects of community building and alternative history writing, archives are a way to tell a story otherwise, and to insist it keeps getting told. Radical archives and archiving resist, recreate, and reimagine. An archive, moreover, is ever only partial. This is a reminder that any pretense to the 'whole story' is the God's Eye fallacy that Haraway warned us about (Haraway, 1988). Admitting our partiality keeps us accountable. Seeing our omissions keeps us striving to do better. Knowing we are never getting the whole story keeps us curious, and hopefully humble.

This collection re-performs selections from three live events staged in 2016, 2017 and 2018 in Sydney, Australia, as a living archive. Contrary to the trend of documenting everything, these events were not recorded and not officially photographed. Moreover, hacking was happening both prior to and beyond the dates of the events themselves, in the form of community building, conversation, retreating, gathering, art-making, reading together, eating together—all the while connecting across neighbourhoods and disciplines but also continents and oceans. Other parts of the Hacking series have been archived in other ways already. For example, hacks from the 2018 event now comprise a special issue of *Australian Feminist Studies*, while Kathryn Yusoff's 2016 hack seeded her book *A Billion Black Anthropocenes or None* (2018). Other hackers opted not to deposit their work in this archive. In its incompleteness, then, this book only tells part of the story. In its re-situation and re-presentation as digital and paper text, it hacks the original performances too—inviting new associations, new relations, and different uptakes with different publics. While this archive holds material souvenirs of those events, we hope it is also "an archive of feelings" (Cvetkovich 2003)—tenuously holding the energies and affects that formed the events' atmospherics. As many participants have told us, the feeling of being part of the hack was just as vital as its content.

We hope that some of this is captured and recast through the argument, augury, poetry, elegy, essay, image, and video gathered here. These contributions suggest alternative understandings of the shifting relationships between humans and nature. Scholars, artists and activists from environmental humanities and related areas of social, political and cultural studies offer a reminder of the entanglements of race, sexuality, gender, coloniality, class, and species in all of our earthly terraformings. Here, Anthropocene politics are staged as both urgent and playful, and insist that the personal is also planetary.

This collection is also an invitation to others to find a home in *Hacking*, and learn with its archive. This archive is centrifugal, moving outwards in excess of itself. Through experimentation in processes of collective thinking, learning, listening, and

Astrida Neimanis

mentoring, a key driver and lesson of *Hacking the Anthropocene* has been the insistence on building communities in difference. *Hacking* is a commitment to making places where one can seek and find fellow travellers; it is a live/digital/fleshy/textual place where one might not be the only one in the room who feels compelled to intervene, to interrupt, to insist. *Hacking* is where you will not be only one having to hack it.

These lessons extend well beyond the blip of the Anthropocene's moment. *Hacking* has been forged in a hope for new and innovative ways of torqueing and cutting, of withstanding, and carrying. Its re-performance as living book keeps the question at the heart of these propositions alive: What kinds of alternative futures are activated when the full force of feminist, anticolonial and queer analysis are welcomed? *You belong here.*

Works Cited

Cvetkovich, Ann. (2003). *An Archive of Feelings.* Durham: Duke University Press.

Hamilton, Jennifer Mae and Neimanis, Astrida. (2018). "Composting Feminism and the Environmental Humanities." *Environmental Humanities.* 10.2, 501–527.

Haraway, Donna. (2015). "Anthropocene, Capitalocene, Plantationocene, Chthulucene: Making Kin." *Environmental Humanities.* 6, 159-165.

Haraway, Donna. (1988). "Situated Knowledges: The Science Question in Feminism and the Privilege of Partial Perspective." *Feminist Studies.* 14. 3, 575-599.

Jackson, Zakkiyah. (2020). *Becoming Human: Matter and Meaning in an Antiblack World.* New York: NYU Press.

McKittrick, Katherine, Ed. (2015). *Sylvia Wynter: On Being Human as Praxis.* Durham: Duke University Press.

Yusoff, Kathryn. "Towards the Idea of a Black Anthropocene" *Feminist, Queer, Anticolonial Propositions for Hacking the Anthropocene* (Sydney: Sydney University, April 8, 2016), Keynote Lecture.

Yusoff, Kathryn. (2018). *A Billion Black Anthropocenes or None.* Minneapolis: University of Minnesota Press.

Part 1: Hacking the Anthropocene (2016)

1 Heat and Light and Water: Resistance Through Fiction[1]

Ellen van Neerven

I shift my body and our shoulders brush. We don't find each other. Then I feel her foot tangle around mine and she puts her arm around me.

'Two worlds?'

'I don't know if...' I move away. 'You're not ...' I can't offend her.

'What you expected?' She's getting used to the patterns of speech. 'Humans never see what's coming. Everything is seasonal, cyclical, dependent on environment and weather conditions. Would I love you in the winter, when my toes are frost? Would I love you in the summer, when the wind comes tumbling on me?'

To understand, I give myself the first question. What is a plant? A plant is a living organism. A plant has cell walls with cellulose and characteristically they obtain most of the world's molecular energy and are the basis of most of the world's ecologies, especially on land. Plants are one of the two main groups into which all living things have been traditionally divided; the other is animals. the division goes back at least as far as Aristotle, who distinguished between plants which generally do not move, and animals which often are mobile to catch their food.

The second question is harder. It is: What is a human?

Notes

1   Ellen van Neerven, "Water" in *Heat and Light* (Brisbane: University of Queensland Press, 2014) 96-97.

2   Deep Time, Deep Tissue

Helen Moore

For L

Here on the altar to multi-dimensional experience
I'm prostrate and naked (from the waist veiled
with a towel), face ensconced in a leatherette crescent
through which I may disappear

>   Your fingers beginning cool, now radiate the Sun
>   into layers of dermis, subcutaneous fat
>   towards the deeper muscle, at first following the grain
>   working with awareness, a mental

>   Gray's Anatomy (all red-raw & flayed!) and your honed
>   sense of intuition. Slowly, where your deft hands
>   press, my body's armour is assuaged – those knots
>   tight as rivets, these flat metallic plates

>   tensioned as if to snap, these blades tempered
>   bands of steel. Time expanding and warmth in
>   oily kneading
>   start to release the stress and toxins, which life
>   in the Anthropocene engenders in our being

>   ...

Much later I'll sob like a child
a stream of dammed emotion gushing out
which left me feeling lighter, as if
I really had shouldered a burden

>   but for now I float – am foetus
>   deep sea mammal
>   first bubble of life
>   in some primordial lagoon

This aching body that at times
I've hated, softens as its contours roll
this body formed from dust of stars

(ah, the energy rippling through us now!)

Deep time, deep tissue –
eyes form black holes. Sometimes I'm dark matter
drawing everything towards me, swallowing it in
(the way Nut swallows the Sun)
making follicles, cells, poems

This 'me' rapidly collapsing, this 'me'
a mere speck, a gleam in Time's eye
yet developed and refined
over millions of years
in our symbiotic home

• • •

Earth, this home that awed
our brave-new astronauts –

wild, animate planet
set in cosmic velvet –

inestimable worth, curves
drifting blue and white

• • •

O, Anthropocene
period of consequences!

In a pinch of geological time our minds
have made deserts of grasslands
dead-zones in oceans, have cut away
vast sections of rainforest 'lung'
erasing cultures of birds, animals, people
eroding soils elaborated for millennia
We knowing humans
disrupting the grand cycles

of biology, chemistry, geology, knowingly persist
in filling the atmosphere with gases

...

which trap the Sun's rays
melting glaciers, turning seas acidic

...

and where our ice-sheets melt
prospect for yet more of Gaia's bitter blood.

O, obscene era
this is an emergency!

...

We breathe, releasing the enormity
of this awareness. How I love

and thank you, dearest Body! You
ancient, four-zoaed temple

open to the skies and aligned to Polaris –
hub around which all other stars

wheel. In whatever mortal span
that remains, help me to navigate

this crisis in our evolution, to stay
with what others have begun

millions of cells rising
in and for our life-source, Earth

willing Ecozoa's birth

from ECOZOA (Permanent Publications, 2015)

3   at home with the alien that I am

Vicki Kirby

Among the many political concerns that demand our attention one of the most pressing in contemporary times is the
speed of environmental degradation, the massive and ongoing
destruction of habitat, and the cascade of species loss that now
amounts to a cataclysm. The Anthropocene, as the name suggests, has been mooted to describe the violence of this human
activity whose effects are said to be legible as a distinct geological stratum. And yet for me, there remains a niggling unease
in the way this judgement identifies the human as culprit and
perpetrator, *the* causal agent who exercises almost unilateral
power and control over its unwitting object and victim - nature.
What concerns me here are the almost automatic discriminations and assumptions which this conviction promotes. Although
it may feel right, and there is certainly an understandable and
quite satisfying need to out a perpetrator and defend a victim,
my sense is that this morality tale of action versus helpless passivity hides a more complex, perverse, and potentially more fascinating story about the implications of ecology (*oikos*/house).
For those who acknowledge climate change as an unfolding
catastrophe, whether the cause is deemed anthropogenic or
not, we are used to hearing that the salve that might better protect life from such extreme assaults must work to recognize the
entangled interdependence of existence. In other words, we will
surely appreciate that existence is an involvement and no entity
can enjoy a life that is independent and autonomous. Indeed,
any entity will already entail an ecology of other creatures both
within and without, and to such an extent that, as we increasingly witness with soil or animal biomes, decisions about how to
live will be a community affair. To put this another way, we don't
need psychoanalysis to complicate the classical belief in a self-
conscious subject who makes its own decisions. If we accept that
our very own, individual, decision-making processes and moods

emerge from neurological structures in the large bowel that are biome dependent, then the site of self is no longer simply cerebral – it appears *thoroughly* corporeal. Given this sense of ecological complicity, we are left to wonder about the nature of this deciding "who."

And yet, if we return to the scene of culprit versus victim and its segregation of author (human) from authored (nature), it seems there is a need to disavow or even repress the real complicities and complexities of ecological entanglement in order to justify this misguided representation. Here we return to Cartesianism, where the site of self is the rational mind, and the body/nature - the mind's unthinking other - is understood as its material support. Importantly, a significant legacy of feminist research has mounted an enduring critique of this style of reasoning because it effects a devaluation of matter, the body, nature, otherness, the feminine as the repository of comparative incapacity. Further, this masculinist logic understands the subject as a creature divided from itself - I am my mind, I have a body – and we recuperate this same logic when we say that the human exists *in* a context, an ecology, which is different from itself. Of course, we could reject these discriminations and argue that woman/the feminine is not closer to nature, or we could argue that woman is, indeed, closer to nature and is therefore more benign, caring and empathically oriented. Unfortunately, both strategies leave the terms of this adjudication intact, whereas my aim is to question the segregationist logic that underpins them both.

What happens if, following Gilbert Simondon, we argue that an ecology (nature) individuates *itself*; in other words, if we suggest that it is in the nature of nature to be cultural, political, human – to argue, contest and re-present itself by way of all its diverse morphological instantiations and strategic options? This would imply that an individual of whatever sort is *inherently* ecological, and not simply because it exists among an aggregation of separate and entirely other entities. Put this way, no creature or process is simply exterior to any other, just as no behaviour can be isolated from another as straightforwardly good or bad.

But what do we do about the ethics of such a messy situation? In short, how should we proceed? It is easy to encourage the sort of feel-good condemnation of human exceptionalism on the one hand, as if anthropocentrism's pomposity, myopia and murderous self-absorption can be diagnosed and thereby dispatched with a convenient *mea culpa*. However, this gesture of atonement and repair on the one hand feels strangely disingenuous when it is human exceptionalism that is leveraged all over again in the questionable belief that the sole agent of responsible oversight, the only one who can take reparative action and engineer environmental repair, is the human subject as master of ceremonies. Can we be satisfied with this familiar tale of sinners and saviours, powerful and powerless, as if the way to engage ethical quandaries is by dividing "us" from "them"; as if all the lessons we learned about the violence of identitarian politics that pits competing agents in agonistic confrontation in other arenas has no relevance in this one?

But how to think this muddle? Jacques Derrida helps me here with his notoriously misread aphorism, "no outside text," no outside metaphysics, no outside logocentrism, no outside phallogocentrism, indeed, no outside anthropocentrism. For a reader unfamiliar with the riddles and possibilities that hide within such seemingly depressing assertions it probably sounds as if I'm making things worse. Does this mean we're stuck? Trapped? Doomed to perform the righteous violence of our self–importance forever and a day without the possibility of escape? No exit from the horrors of a power play that loves to identify, to find value by devaluing – just as anthropocentrism does, but also, and this is the perversity here, just as the critique of anthropocentrism does?

Through a grammatological reading, the centring of man, or the human, is effectively *de*centred as an entity among others, an entity whose obvious superiority and importance is submerged and dissolved in the ecological gravitas that finds the centre everywhere and nowhere. The morphological instantiation of every creature involves a certain centring, and yet this is a process that is not straightforwardly locatable. I think that the

Vicki Kirby

identity of *anthropos* is a question, a question about what goes into making an identity appear as such. If *anthropos* isn't what we thought it was because the agential is dispersed – or, to put this another way, when perceived as local it still carries within it non-local intrigues - then where we begin to do politics will always involve the global. For example, how we decide on any tactic, any particular point of entry, will open within a field of forces that remains subject to those same forces. Consequently, if I "decide" to engage environmental issues, my point isn't that it doesn't matter, why bother, but that I am already authored by an ecological field that moves me to this, just as it moves another in a different way that I might perceive as murderous.

Although I believe the shape of discourses that encourage environmental engagement and activism are necessary and increasingly compelling, I at least want to entertain the pos-sibility of thinking about the ecology in terms which are even more comprehensive. What happens if we place *anthropos*, the human, under erasure, or if we ask what a centre might be in a universe that can have none? Or to go another route, can we concede that even responses to natural catastrophe that beggar belief – climate change denial, the triumphalism that can moti-vate destructive land-clearing or mining practices, the failure to appreciate the deep serenity and ancient legacies of old growth forests and so on, must also be intrinsic to an enlarged and more intricate and involved ecology that none of us control outright. If the ecology isn't a surround, a context *within which* we live, if it is the very stuff of what and who we are, then our separation from a benign and happy nature that we can choose to destroy or save may be seriously misleading.

What if nature is duplicitous, treacherous, self-deceived and self-deceiving, even suicidal at times? But also caring, self-sac-rificing, empathic, deeply thoughtful and generous. And what if the difference between the two isn't always clear because an opportunity from one perspective is a mortal cul-de-sac from another. In other words, what if nature's ecology involves the dis-persed, often contradictory forces of push and pull that consti-tute the very stuff of who I am? What if it's in the nature of nature to be political? *In sum, what if culture was really nature all along?* If we are offended by the suggestion then perhaps we need to ask ourselves why. Nature isn't passive and prescriptive in this description, but thoroughly agential, and we cannot objectify its force as other to our own subjectivity. Of course, nature isn't just one thing, but then, why should it be? Is anything autonomous, easily described, and straightforwardly itself? Importantly, we are not prevented from taking action against what we perceive as the destructiveness of others. However, if our goal is the defence, nourishment and care of the ecology, it might be a salutary exercise to consider that perhaps there is no outside this ecology, and that the enemy is within it, and therefore, within us.

4 Volatizing Bouquet

Stephanie Springgay

Inhale

My contribution to Hacking the Anthropocene was a smelly one. I installed an industrial sized diffuser next to the podium. The diffuser was armed with a chemically produced scent that mimicked the smell of freshly mown grass. Typically, a diffuser of this size would be used in hotel lobbies or large corporate spaces and the scent would be diluted. As the 'hackers' presented their short papers, films, and artistic interventions, the conference space filled with a potent aroma. People gagged. Some felt dizzy. Many kept looking around for the source of the odorous penetration. My hack contained no paper presentation. It was left unannounced except for my name, hack title, and an ambiguous description written in the program.

This short paper, written almost two years later, offers a contextualization of my hack. To commence, I site a few artistic examples that use smell to disrupt occularcentrism, situating the work in the broader sensory turn in contemporary art practice. Further, I connect the ways that smells and the other bodily senses have been historically neglected in knowledge production, to critiques of posthumanism that disregard discussions about race. By way of conclusion, I reflect on my choice of cut grass as a scent, plant communication, and *Volatizing Bouquet* as affective, propositional, and intensive.

Olafactory art

The sensory turn in artistic practice includes diverse projects including smell maps, smell walks, perfumery experiments, and public installations where audiences encounter and experience artwork through their noses (as opposed to their eyes). Smell is used to evoke memory and emotions, as a political gesture, and to innovatively question and challenge the reliance on vision in exhibition spaces. There is a tendency to regard the senses as purely phenomenological and neutral, but how smells are mediated and encountered are influenced by social and cultural forces. As such, odors are highly political. As Drobinck writes "no act of perception is a pure or unmediated event" (1). Smell, much like taste and touch, has been excluded from aesthetic perception. Smell is often conceived of as merely biological and thus not a legitimate form of cognition or understanding. Olfactory art challenges the aesthetic realm opening up visual art to the subjective, the immediate, and the bodily.

An example of a project that discretely incorporated smells in order to unsettle an otherwise visual space was Diane Borsato's *Cloud* (Springgay, 2016). In this performative piece, Borsato asked 24 friends and colleagues to join her at an art opening at a small commercial gallery wearing a Gardenia corsage. The 24 participants mingled with the gallery patrons and the heavy scent from the Gardenia, warmed by the crowded room, quickly became overbearing and toxic. Clara Ursitti has used smell in a number of her projects, including the installation the *Smell of Fear*. In this piece, audiences are assaulted with a chemically produced scent – body odor mixed with perfume – when they walked by a scent dispenser (which looked like a speaker) in a small gallery room. In another project, I presented a performance lecture on the *Politics and Pedagogy of Smell* to a room of more than 50 people. As I spoke, the audience chopped 200 pounds of onion, which I had provided along with knives and cutting boards when they entered the lecture hall. This was followed by a smell graffiti workshop, where participants used personal atomizers to odorize public spaces using scents such as buttered popcorn, rain shower, and warm breeze (Springgay, 2014).

More-than-human: Hacking humanism's constructions of race and smell

The more-than-human emerges at time in scholarly debates that seek to challenge the centrality of the human subject, taxonomies of knowledge, and the rigid distinctions between nature and culture (Springgay and Truman 2017a; Springgay and Truman

Stephanie Springgay

2018). Chen argues that animacy has been historically aligned to the category of the human (24). At the top of the animacy taxonomy are masculine, heteronormative, able bodies, with intact capacities. As you move down the schema, as bodies and things become less agentic, they become less animate. Race, disability, and gender, for example, fall at the lower end of the animacy taxonomy. This taxonomy, Chen argues, is a contributing factor in dehumanization, where qualities valued as 'human' are removed (24). These taxonomic logics pervade our understanding of sensory knowing. Vision, which is associated with rational, objective thought remains at the top of the hierarchy, while touch, taste, and smell, senses affiliated with the body are understood as too subjective, too immediate, and as such not part of the rational order (Springgay 2011a; 2011b; Springgay and Zaliwska). Humanism, in fact, is defined by a lack of smells. The clean and proper human body is one that is pure, deodorized, and not leaky. Smells have moral and political underpinnings, where to be human means to be transformed into an odorless subject. The animal, the immigrant, the slave, the Indigenous carry with them redolent tropes of heavy scent, which have been used by White supremacy to facilitate abjection and dehumanization (Manalansan 41). Cleanliness, including how one smells, polices particular bodies "where purity is maintained through the expulsion of the polluting member" (Hyde 55). Smells are powerful racial markers, where bodies, food, and neighbourhoods become denigrated, classified, and/or exoticized through sticky aromas. Manalansan argues, "the immigrant body is culturally constructed to be the natural carrier and source of undesirable sensory experiences and is popularly perceived to be the site of polluting and negative olfactory signs" (41). Banes contends that the Other's smell "creates an ideological representation of the West as odorless and therefore neutral and the norm" (35). Chen's detailed account of their chemical sensitivity to scents describes how particular bodies are made to feel toxic (24). Public spaces – full of smoke or perfume – can trigger environmental illness for Chen, yet simultaneously it is their racialized, masked body that is rendered as toxic against a White collective norm. Room diffusers, like the one used in my hack, used to deodorize corporate spaces such as hotel lobbies and stores, reinforce systems of classification and exclusion. Corporate branding of scents is a civilizing process that through connoisseurship re-inscribes class and racial hierarchies (Springgay and Truman, 2017b 51).

The dehumanization that defines the Anthropocene is fundamentally entangled with race, settler colonization, and transatlantic slavery (Springgay and Truman 2019). For example, Jackson contends that posthumanism, in its descriptions and theorizing of vitality, remains committed to a particular Euro-Western understanding of humanism (215), or what Sylvia Wynter calls 'Man' (672). For Jackson, and other critical races scholars who engage with posthumanism, the aim is not that people of colour will somehow "gain admittance into the fraternity of Man" that they have always been outside of, the aim is to "displace the order of Man altogether" (672). This means re-thinking posthumanism, not as a politics of inclusion for those enslaved or colonized under liberal humanist ideals, but as a strategy of transforming *humanism*. As affect and sensory scholars, we must then become committed to a politicization of sensation, where smells are never assumed to be natural or neutral. Posthumanism and new materialism must radically undo humanisms sensory taxonomies. As Luciano states, "The most compelling contribution of the new materialisms is not conceptual or analytic, strictly speaking, but sensory. The attempt to attend to the force of liveliness of matter will entail not just a reawakening or redirection of critical attention, but a reorganizing of the senses, departing from the limitations of the Aristotelian model" (np). This requires grappling with affects and matter across different scales including 'data' that is diffuse, porous, and difficult to capture (Springgay and Truman, 2017c 204).

The scent of grass

Reflecting back on my hack, all of these concerns were circulating as I created my intervention. A scent that mimicked freshly mown grass was selected because of readings I had been doing

Stephanie Springgay

at the time on plant communication. The smell of freshly mown grass is actually a distress call. When attacked, plants emit chemical compounds to communicate to other 'creatures' the threat of parasitic invasion. According to Hustak and Myers the plant "synthesizes and releases a concentrated plume of volatile chemicals that can disperse widely" (99). Volatile refers to a substance that is easily evaporated and also one that undergoes rapid and unpredictable change. Smell is not inherent in grass but produced through traumatic encounters. Machine severs grass; odor penetrates and affects human and nonhuman bodies, attesting to plants' sensuous dexterity. Plants use chemical ecology to communicate, express, and involve themselves in a world making. Hustak and Myers write that "this volatility gets read as a kind of vocality, a way of speaking in a chemical vocabulary" (100). However, they note that scientists are reluctant to use terms like speaking and sentient when describing and writing about chemical ecologies relying on Anthropocentric models that continue to position plants mechanically. Hustak and Myers suggest that an involutionary reading of plant communication is necessary, where plants signals and syntax do not need to conform to human representations of language. Instead an involutionary reading asks questions about how sentience and sensory affects are "transduced within and among bodies" (105). The air circulation system sucked up the grass odor and pumped it back into the room. The noxious scent thickened and clung to human and nonhuman bodies. If humanism and the Anthropocene are materialized through affective and sensory ecologies, then posthumanism requires a form of *Volatizing Bouquet* – its complexity, intimacy, evanescence, and inability to be contained.

Works Cited

Banes, S. (2007). "Olfactory performances." In S. Banes & A. Lepecki (Eds.). *The Senses in Performance*. NY: Routledge. 29-37.

Chen, M.Y. (2012). *Animacies: Biopolitics, Racial Mattering, and Queer Affect*. Durham, NC: Duke University Press.

Drobnick, J. (Ed.). (2006). *The Smell Culture Reader.* New York, NY: Berg.

Hustak, C & Myers, N. (2012). "Involutionary Momentum: Affective Ecologies and the Sciences of Plant/Insect Encounters." *differences* 23(3), 74-118.

Hyde, (2006). "Offensive bodies." In J. Drobnick (Ed.). *The Smell Culture Reader.* New York, NY: Berg. 53-58.

Jackson, Z. I. (2015). "Outer Worlds: The Persistence of Race in Movement 'Beyond the Human'." *Gay and Lesbian Quarterly (GLQ)*, 21(2-3), 215-218.

Luciano, D. (2015). In C. Roudeau, "How the Earth Feels: A Conversation with Dana Luciano." *Transatlantica* 1, http://transatlantica.revues.org/7362.

Manalansan, M. (2006). "Immigrant Lives and the Politics of Olfaction in the Global City." In J. Drobnick (Ed.). *The Smell Culture Reader.* NY: Berg. 41-52.

Springgay, S. (2011a). "'The Chinatown Foray' as Sensational Pedagogy." *Curriculum Inquiry* 41, 636–656.

Springgay, S. (2011b). "The Ethicoaesthetics of Affect and a Sensational Pedagogy." *Journal of the Canadian Association for Curriculum Studies* 9(1), 66-82.

Springgay, S. (2014). "Olfaction: On Learning through the Nose." *Visual Arts Research* 40(1), 127-128.

Springgay, S. (2016). "Meditating with Bees: Weather Bodies and a Pedagogy of Movement." In N. Snaza, D. Sonu, S. E. Truman, & Z. Zaliwska (Eds.). *Pedagogical matters: New materialism and curriculum studies.* New York, NY: Peter Lang. 59-74.

Springgay, S. & Truman, S. E. (2017a). "Stone Walks: inhuman animacies and queer archives of feeling." *Discourse: Studies in the Cultural Politics of Education* 38(6), 851-863.

Springgay, S. & Truman, S. E. (2017b). "A Transmaterial Approach to Walking Methodologies: Embodiment, Affect and a Sonic Art Performance." *Body & Society. Body & Society* 23(4), 27-58.

Springgay, S. & Truman, S. E. (2017). "On the Need for Methods Beyond Proceduralism: Speculative Middles, (In) tensions, and Reponse-ability in Research." *Qualitative Inquiry* 24(3), 203-214.

Stephanie Springgay

Springgay, S. & Truman, S. E. (2018). *Walking methodologies in a more-than-human world*. New York, NY: Routledge.

Springgay, S. & Truman, S. E. (2019). "Queering Temporalities, Activating QTBIPOC Subjectivities and World-makings: Walking research-creation." *MAI: FEMINISM & VISUAL CULTURE*. *https:// maifeminism.com/walking-research-creation-qtbipoc-temporalities-and-world-makings/*

Springgay, S. & Zaliwska, Z. (2016). "Learning to be Affected: Matters of Pedagogy in the Artists' Soup Kitchen." *Educational Philosophy and Theory* 49(3), 273-283.

Wynter, S. (2003). "Unsettling the Coloniality of Being/ Power/Truth/Freedom: Towards the Human, After Man, it's overrepresentation--An Argument." *CR: The New Centennial Review* 3(3), 257-337.

5   Animist Lures: Arts of Witness

Deborah Bird Rose and Thom van Dooren

Talk, our human chatter, our great fascination with words, has the potential to take over. At times it threatens to crowd out the liveliness of the biosphere with which we are so concerned when we talk about the Anthropocene. Of course, worlds and words are far from being unrelated concerns. And yet, when the preponderance of ponderance focuses on the latter, we worry that the world itself—along with the very real and rapid unravelling of it that the term 'Anthropocene' was coined to describe—slips from view.[1]

Our "hack" aims to draw attention away from important but limited discussions about the suitability of a word—its omissions, erasures and violences—away from the often "meta", zoomed out and abstracted processes that it describes, and instead to throw out some lures that draw attention to the fleshy particularity, the beauty and responsiveness, of earth others—many of whom are in peril.

We want to turn toward the world and to celebrate it in its lively, radiant, responsive, mattering, diversity. Using words, we hope to turn away from word-dominance. In this brief offering, we condense two aspects of earthly particularity. The first is the responsiveness of life – the fact that the biosphere is replete with sensitivities. The second takes up one kind of sensitivity, one lure – that of beauty.

Response[2]

The ecologist Paul Shepard proposed that 'we need to discover how to cherish the world of life on its own terms'. He readily acknowledged that some humans and some cultures already do this; his words were directed toward the many, perhaps the majority, who seem oblivious to the vivid reality of the nonhuman world (Shepard, 12).

Through our own efforts to cherish the world on its own terms, we have become captivated by its lively responsiveness. More accurately, by the *multiplicity* of living kinds woven through with so many different forms of perceiving, striving, desiring, sensing, adapting, communicating and responding. These include a range from the obvious examples of intentional, mindful, affective behavior in the animal kingdom, through to the less familiar forms of "'[c]hoice', 'discrimination', 'memory', 'learning', 'instinct', 'judgment', and 'adaptation' that biochemist Daniel Koshland describes in bacterial worlds (qtd. in Margulis and Sagan, 219). Or, in a similar vein, there are the many varieties of sentience and agency being increasingly described amongst plants who sensitively detect and respond to their environments in adaptive and communicative ways: for example, warding off herbivores by synthesizing chemical deterrents or even by releasing other chemicals that alert potential predators to the presence of problematic grazing insects (Hall; Hustak and Myers; Trewavas; Marder).

Put simply, ours is a world in which all life forms—from the smallest cell to the largest redwood—are involved in diverse forms of adaptive, generative, responsiveness. This responsiveness may happen in the immediacy of the moment (as two albatrosses sing and dance to form a pair bond), it may happen through drawn out developmental processes (as 'parent' trees nurture their youngsters by transferring nutrients to them through their entangled roots)(Wohlleben), or it may happen over evolutionary time frames that remake entwined morphological and behavioral forms to better inhabit their worlds. However it happens though, life is saturated in diverse forms of purposeful attentiveness and responsiveness.[3]

In paying attention to these processes, we aim to *cultivate and expand our own modes of attentiveness*, to develop—but also to reclaim and nurture existing—"sensitivities to earth others" (Plumwood 2002, 177). The natural sciences *can* be an ally here, as can be the diverse was of knowing and living of a range of other people from farmers and hunters, to Indigenous peoples and artists. Ultimately, what is at stake here is learning how to better see and understand the lively responsiveness of our world, so that we might ourselves cultivate capacities to respond *well*.

Radiant Beauty

The injunction 'to cherish the world *on its own terms'* challenges us to become participants, to be responsive. One aspect of life to which we humans are responsive is beauty. And to be clear: We're not talking about a sublime or Romantic vision.

There is the beauty of form that is shaped by the fluid action of water and wind: the sculpted geomorphology of earth; the interactions between flow and resistance; the places of yielding, and the places of obduracy; minerals in interaction—their colours and compositions; histories inscribed on the face of the earth.

There is the beauty of form that comes from within living things: bilateral symmetry; proportionality; the fit between form and function. These 'endless forms most beautiful', as Charles Darwin called them (Carroll).

There is the beauty of pattern: the waves and ripples, and the light that glitters upon them; circularities and repetitions. And there is the beauty of all this *intersecting* beauty. Meta-beauty is earth's radiance. It forms in connection, rippling in the shimmer of long grass in the wind, or the sudden appearance of the rainbow.

Another radiance is beauty that attracts. Consider, just briefly, the mistletoe whose bright colours attract both pollinators and grazers, calling out for their attentive response. The nectar and berries are loaded with sugars and fats, and flash little birds disperse the berries. The beauty of the tree and its mutualists: everyone who comes to the mistletoe feast leaves nutrients; the tree nurtures itself, its visitors, and its hangers on. Radiance is here in these vertical and horizontal planes, and in the sensorial, energetic and temporal patterns of attraction and fulfilment.[4]

This is the beauty of desire; the beauty that says 'I want you to want me'. It expresses both pattern and connection. Beauty is part of what makes possible the continuity of generations. We see this in so many incredible ways in the 'singular' phenomena of avian courtship: from albatross pairs bobbing and weaving, singing and dancing, on land and in air (van Dooren, 21-45); to birds of paradise with their elaborate plumage (males) engaged in equally elaborate spectacles of sound and movement (De Vos); and the wonderfully ornate constructions with which bowerbirds express their skill and creativity. These acts of beauty-making form an "ethological poetics" (Cooke). This poetics does not need humans to behold it, but rather arises because beauty is part of what life is.

There is a terrible paradox here: a disconnect between the fact that we are able to know so much, and the fact that we are able to protect so little. One example: it is now possible with microscope technologies to look closely at each of the cells that makes up the colourful patterns of butterfly wings, and to study the genes that control the colour and patterning of these cells, and yet the great migratory pathway of monarch butterfly life is imperilled, and so, too, is their future.

In sum: responsiveness is relational; it involves not just knowing but also doing. It involves a kind of response—grounded in close attention—that takes an interest in what matters to another rather than reading one's own positioning on to them (Rose 1999; 2007). It asks how, given the pressing demands of our time, we ourselves are called to respond to others, perhaps to hold open space for the ongoing flourishing of their forms of life. To do what we can to ensure that what matters, matters.

Notes

1   This is not a conventional use of the term "ponderance" but is supported by the *Urban Dictionary*: "Ponderances: Ponderous thoughts to be ponderously pondered. Basically, if there is an adverb, adjective, and verb of ponder, then it stands to reason that there ought to be a noun as well."

2   The ideas offered in this short section have now been developed in more substantial detail in van Dooren and Rose, 1–17; Rose and van Dooren 2016.

3   Val Plumwood explores similarly expansive, more-than-human, forms of intelligence and sentience in Plumwood 2009.

4   For a slightly expanded discussion of mistletoe, see Rose and van Dooren 2016, 123-124.

Works Cited

Carroll, Sean. (2006, 2011). *Endless Forms Most Beautiful: The New Science of Evo Devo and the Making of the Animal Kingdom*. London: Quercus.

Cooke, Stuart. (2017). "What Are the Animals Saying?" *Plumwood Mountain* 4.

De Vos, Rick. (2017). "Extinction in a Distant Land: The Question of Elliot's Bird of Paradise." In *Extinction Studies: Stories of Time, Death and Generations*, edited by Deborah Bird Rose, Thom van Dooren, and Matthew Chrulew. New York: Columbia University Press. 89-116.

Hall, Matthew. (2011). *Plants as Persons: A Philosophical Botany*. Albany, NY: SUNY Press.

Hustak, Carla, and Natasha Myers. (2012). "Involutionary Momentum: Affective Ecologies and the Sciences of Plant/Insect Encounters." *differences* 23, 74–118.

Marder, Michael. (2013). *Plant-Thinking: A Philosophy of Vegetal Life*. New York: Columbia University Press.

Margulis, Lynn, and Dorian Sagan. (1995). *What is Life?* Berkeley and Los Angeles: University of California Press.

Plumwood, Val. (2009). "Nature in the Active Voice." *Australian Humanities Review* 46, 113-129.

Plumwood, Val. (2002). *Environmental Culture: The Ecological Crisis of Reason*. London and New York: Routledge.

Rose, Deborah Bird. (2007)."Recursive Epistemologies and an Ethics of Attention." In *Extraordinary Anthropology: Transformations in the Field*, edited by B Miller. Lincoln: University of Nebraska Press. 88–102.

Rose, Deborah Bird. (1999). "Taking Notice." *Worldviews; Environment, Culture, Religion* 3, 97–103.

Rose, Deborah Bird, and Thom van Dooren. (2016)."Encountering a More-than-Human World: Ethos and the Arts of Witness." In *Routledge Companion to the Environmental Humanities*, edited by Ursula K. Heise, Jon Cristensen, and Michelle Niemann. London: Routledge. 120-128.

Shepard, Paul. (1996). *The Others: How Animals Made Us Human*. Washington D.C.: Island Press.

Trewavas, Anthony. (2002). "Plant Intelligence: Mindless Mastery." *Nature* 415, 841.

van Dooren, Thom. (2014). *Flight Ways: Life and Loss at the Edge of Extinction*. New York: Columbia University Press.

van Dooren, Thom, and Deborah Bird Rose. (2016). "Lively Ethography: Storying Animist Worlds." *Environmental Humanities* 8(1) , 1–17.

Wohlleben, Peter. (2016). *The Hidden Life of Trees*. Translated by Jane Billinghurst. London: William Collins.

6 Extreme Baking: Toward an Anticolonial Ingestion of Hardtack

Lindsay Kelley

Figure 1. Hardtack prepared for and consumed by attendees of Feminist, Queer Anticolonial Propositions for Hacking the Anthropocene. Photo by Lindsay Kelley.

For *Feminist, Queer, Anticolonial Propositions for Hacking the Anthropocene*, I prepared and distributed a wheat-based biscuit called "hard tack," also known as ship's biscuits, seabiscuits, cabin bread, and for WWI Australia New Zealand Army Corps (ANZAC) soldiers, Anzac tiles or wafers. Because hardtack is so durable, examples exist in museum collections around the world, making it one of the few foods available for archival research. In this essay, developed from my short hack titled "Extreme Baking: Toward an anticolonial ingestion of hardtack," I trace a history of hardtack as a key feature in the nutritional environment of colonial expansion. With two related foods, Native American fry bread and Anzac biscuits, I speculate that attending to the usually overlooked taste of wheat and gluten can have decolonizing effects. This is an expanded version of my hack, based on a talk given at *Technicity, Temporality, Embodiment: The 10th International Somatechnics Conference* in Byron Bay a few months after *Hacking the Anthropocene.* I have punctuated the text with recipes for wheat-based biscuits from different historic and cultural contexts. At *Hacking the Anthropocene,* I made this recipe, from *Urban Survival Site*:

Hardtack Recipe

3 cups of white flour

2 teaspoons of salt

1 cup of water

A cookie sheet

A mixing bowl

A knife

A common nail

First, you'll need to preheat your oven to 375°.

Mix the flour and salt together in a bowl.

Gradually mix in the water until you form a dough that doesn't stick to your hands. It will be very sticky at first, but just keep forming it and shaping it until it's not too sticky.

Next, you'll need to use a rolling pin to flatten the dough into a square. Make sure it's no more than half an inch thick or it won't bake well.

Now carefully cut the dough into 9 squares.

Using the nail, make a 4×4 grid of holes in each of the squares.

Put all the pieces on an ungreased cookie sheet and bake them for 30 minutes.

Now turn the squares over and bake for another 30 minutes.

Remove them from the oven and let them cool off.

> Ideally, the hardtack should be just a little brown on each side. Every oven is different and every climate has an effect on baking time, so keep a close eye on them the first time you bake them. You don't want to burn your first batch. (Urban 2017)

Urban Survival Site addresses "preppers" or survivalists--anyone invested in preparedness. Motivations for preparedness vary, and include natural disaster, global war, climate change, and diverse related doomsday scenarios. Preppers care about food, and usually take their culinary cues from militaries past and present. Hardtack is among the oldest military rations, one of the first foods that might be classified as a "meal ready to eat" or MRE. Even though MREs have become much more sophisticated in the centuries since Roman armies carried hardtack, the humble biscuits still appeal to preppers, recipes still circulate, and cupboards are still stocked with this food.

The recipe appeals in its simplicity. No need for the flameless self-heating or vacuum sealing technologies found in today's MREs. All you need is flour, water, and salt. These ingredients are formed into biscuits and baked twice to evaporate as much of the water as possible. For very long sea voyages, the biscuits would have been baked four times to ensure an even longer shelf life. As an educational activity for students, the Australian War Memorial offers a "softer" recipe for hardtack that includes self-raising flour, milk powder, and sugar (below). Recipes without sugar or milk powder last longer.

Hardtack Recipe

Caution: Hard tack is really hard! There are stories of soldiers breaking their teeth on it, so be careful!

Makes six biscuits.

Ingredients

1½ cups self-raising white flour

3 cups self-raising wholemeal flour

5 tablespoons sugar

3 tablespoons milk powder

pinch salt

1 cup water

Equipment

Large mixing bowl

Mixing spoon

Board and rolling pin

Baking tray

Method

Preheat the oven to 180C.

Place dry ingredients in a large bowl and mix together.

Make a well in the centre and add the water. Mix together until an even dough is formed.

Turn the dough onto a floured board and knead for a few minutes. Shape the dough into a ball and let rest for half an hour.

Divide the dough into three and then roll each ball into thick 1cm sheets.

Cut the rolled sheet of dough into 9 cm squares, using the edge of a steel ruler, rather than a knife. This pressing action helps to join the top and bottom surfaces of the biscuit and will improve the "lift" in baking.

Now make a regular pattern of holes in each biscuit, five holes across by five holes down (25 holes in all). The ideal tool to use to make these holes is a cotton bud with the cotton wool cut off or the thick end of a bamboo skewer. Push it through to the bench, twist slightly and withdraw. (Some historians claim that each biscuit had 49 holes.)

Place on a slightly greased baking tray, being careful that the biscuits are not touching. Form a wall around the outside edge with scrap dough. This will stop the outside edges of the biscuits from burning.

Bake on the centre shelf for 30-40 minutes or until golden brown. Be careful not to burn them!

Leave the biscuits on a cooling rack until they harden. Or switch off the oven and return the biscuits to the oven until it becomes cool. (Make Hard Tack 2017)

Hardtack is so stable that it is possible to visit centuries-old examples in museum collections around the world. For example, hardtack dating from 1852 is on display at the Military Museum of Denmark (see Figure 2). In 2016, I visited hardtack holdings in the UK, Australia, and New Zealand, finding that museums collected hardtack not only to document historic military rations, but also to archive its creative repurposing as artistic canvas, photo frames, or even postcards. Museums also display hardtack replicas, made from edible and inedible substances. For example, replica foods were created for the New Zealand National Army Museum's exhibition *Food Glorious Food: An Army Marches On Its Stomach*, and the IWM includes replicas in its display vitrines as well.

Figure 2. "The World's Oldest Ship's Biscuit". Photo by Paul Cziko CC-BY-SA.

This is the Jacka Bakery in the UK (see Figure 3), where the Pilgrims who travelled to Wampanoag territory, what is now New England, bought their hard tack. The English separatists wintered over in their ships, surviving (or not) on their rations. These included, and by the end of their voyage, were predominantly, hardtack from Jacka Bakery. The Pilgrims, the Conquistadors, the Dutch East Indies traders and other seafaring colonisers and settlers: their bodies were all made of hard tack. Hardtack

Lindsay Kelley

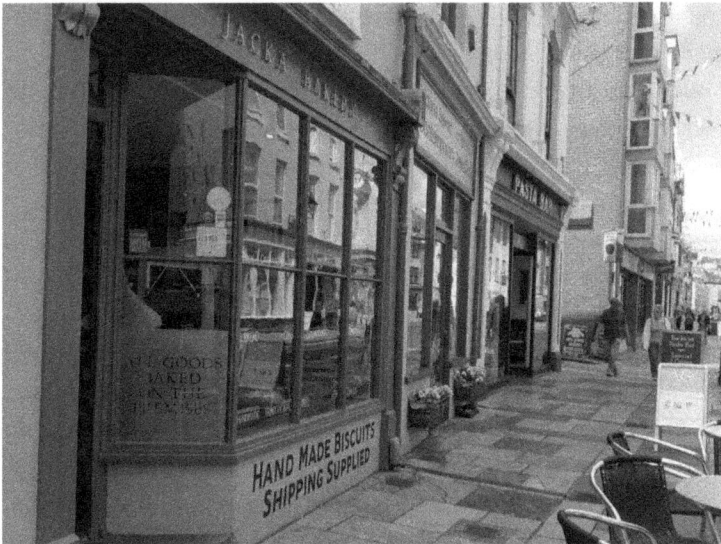
Figure 3. The Jacka Bakery in Plymouth, UK. Photo by Lindsay Kelley.

is a substance of conquest. As the food that conquering bodies were exposed to, hardtack was at times the only component of the nutritional environment of European colonial expansion. Hardtack made conquest possible.

Hannah Landecker looks to nutritional epigenetics to articulate food as an environment--food is a form of molecular exposure. In Landecker's analysis of nutritional epigenetics, the shift from understanding metabolism as an engine channeling transubstantiated caloric energy to understanding the relational responsiveness of the body to its nutritional surroundings suggests that "if the body is open to environment, then it is open to environmental intervention" (Landecker 2011, 179). This idea that the body is open to environment is a core contribution of epigenetics, a relatively new area of enquiry in biology that interrogates changes in organisms caused after birth and across generations by modifications to gene expression. Epigenetics is that which is over, outside of, around genetics. Eating exposes bodies to a nutritional environment. Eating could change and reconstitute everything about the body, not just fat or muscle, but also genetic expression. How might analysis of colonial expansion shift when hardtack is understood to be the nutritional environment of colonial violence?

With hard tack we are reminded that the gut, as Elizabeth Wilson puts it, is "an organ of mind" (Wilson 2015). We find reference to the ways that ships biscuits recall qualities of the mind in Shakespeare's *As You Like It*. Touchstone, local fool and jester, has a "brain, Which is as dry as the remainder biscuit / After a voyage" (*As You Like It*, 2.7.38-40). A biscuit brain is addled, confused, thrown together.

When we eat biscuits and crackers, we taste the places where and manner in which wheat and humans have travelled together. We taste the movement of wheat from the fertile crescent to Europe to the Americas and Australia. We taste the consolidation of cultivated wheat species into common wheat, *Triticum aestivum* (Head et al. 2012). We taste an ancient military standard for survival and for healthy digestion. Today we prefer to eat our military rations sweetly, as with Anzac biscuits and fry bread. Annemarie Mol writes an eating body, finding that eating bodies in Western practice and theory have been neglected by the philosophies that were produced in conversation with colonial expansion and divided nature from culture (Mol, 2008). What if we remembered what colonizing bodies ate? Those who eat a traditional Western diet do remember the diets of conquest, if only by maintaining wheat as a bland baseline staple across all major meals.

At *Feminist, Queer Anticolonial Propositions for Hacking the Anthropocene*, everyone who wanted a piece of hardtack eventually sat holding their small biscuit, sometimes making an effort to eat it, sometimes not. After collectively holding the biscuits for some time, I asked, "What might you do to inscribe an eating body with the piece of hardtack you hold in your hands? How might you eat this biscuit? Perhaps soaked in tea, with broth, perhaps shredded?"

Hard tack resists. Hard tack resists time, resists acts of eating, resists the teeth and the throat and the soft lining of our guts. Can ingesting military rations be an act of political and physical resistance? The Diné (Native American Navajo Nation) would

Lindsay Kelley

Figure 4. A tintype of Augustus B. Hayes in a hardtack frame, from the National Museum of American History, Kenneth E. Behring Center. Photo Lindsay Kelley.

say yes. The same year that Augustus Bigelow Hayes wrote on this piece of hardtack (see Figure 4), 1864, the Navajo people were deported from their land in what is now Arizona and forced to walk 500 kilometers to eastern New Mexico. This is called the Long Walk.

Frybread #16 Southwest

3 cups unbleached flour, sifted

½ cup dry powdered milk

2 quarts oil for frying

½ tsp salt

½ cup warm water

1 tbsp baking powder

Mix ingredients in large bowl and knead until soft dough forms, but not sticky. Don't overwork the dough. Brush a tablespoon of oil over the dough. Allow to rise or rest for 20 minutes to 2 hours in a bowl. Cover pan or kettle, when it reaches 375 °F or low boil. Pull egg sized pieces of dough off and quickly pull and pat them into plate sized rounds. They should be thick in the middle and ¼ inch thick at the edges. Gently ease into hot oil, one at a time. Turn the bread once. Allow about 2 minutes per side. When done, remove, shake and place on paper towel to dry. (Miller 2014, 86)

In 1868, the Diné returned to their land. Navajo histories of fry bread locate its origin in these years of deportation and intern-

Fry bread from Tacobe in Denver. Photo by Lindsay Kelley.

ment. Fry bread was invented from the military rations the people received in exile: lard, flour, salt, sugar, leavening agents. From these humble origins, fry bread has become one of the most ubiquitous and celebrated Native American foods, a staple at every pow wow in North America, the critical ingredient in the Indian Taco, and perhaps the only food consistently eaten and celebrated across almost every American Indian First Nation. For writer and filmmaker Sherman Alexie, "Frybread is the story of our survival" (Miller 2008). Frybread vendor Leonard Chee claims that "A powwow won't function without fry-bread" because "frybread connects tribes." He goes on to say that despite and perhaps because of its terrible health attributes, "Frybread is Navajo life" (Miller 2008). Suzan Shown Harjo tried to dampen Indian ardor for fry bread, writing that "It's the connecting dot between healthy children and obesity, hypertension, diabetes, dialysis, blindness, amputations, and slow death. If frybread were a movie, it would be hard-core porn. No redeeming qualities. Zero nutrition" (Miller 2008). Her campaign against fry bread didn't gain much traction, and it is easy to understand why when we hear from historian Cynthia Detterick-Piñeda, who writes, "to some, fry bread is a sacred tradition. It is to be consumed by the people until the earth has again become purified"

Lindsay Kelley

(Piñeda, 2017). Waiting for purity will be a long wait. Let's hope we find ways of cooperating with our wheat crop in the meantime.

Anzac biscuits, No 2

1 cup each of rolled oats, sugar and coconut

1 tablespoon syrup

3/4 cup flour

2 tablespoons butter

1 teaspoon bicarbonate of soda (dissolved in 2 tablespoons boiling water)

Method

Melt butter.

Add syrup to dissolved soda and water. Combine with melted butter.

Mix dry ingredients and stir in liquid.

Place small balls on hot buttered tray and bake in moderate oven.

Lift out carefully with a knife as they are soft till cold.
(Anzac Biscuit Recipes 2017)

Like fry bread, Anzac biscuits were created in dialogue with military rations, in this case the hard, durable "Anzac tile" described by eaters at for example Gallipoli, who noted that the consumption of military ration hardtack biscuits was a significant cause of dental injuries. The Anzac biscuit's hardness and durability connect postwar domestic eaters with food observed on the battlefield.

Like *Hacking the Anthropocene* participants, Adelaide food critic Tony Love also conducted a taste test of Anzac tiles. For Love, the Anzac tile is "bloody tough going," and in its toughness, is "true." Love begins by declaring that the sweet Anzac biscuit "glamorises the genuine article and skews how we imagine those soldiers survived the battlefield," but after his experiments with hard tack, Love trails off with "Can anyone bake me up a batch of sweet and sticky Anzac biscuits …" (Love 2016). Sugar seems safe. Golden syrup insulates us from the horrors of war; we want to cocoon our far away loved ones and war dead in thick gestational syrup, and we imagine that sweetness will solve something through comfort. Love wants sweet and sticky Anzac biscuits, and he wants someone else to make them for him.

Sian Supski distinguishes Anzac biscuits from Scottish oat cake predecessors, declaring that "the originality of Anzac biscuits is the use of golden syrup" (Supski 2006, 52). The earliest published recipes for Anzac biscuits date from the 1920s, after the war had ended. Precursors to Anzac biscuits might have been sent to the front, but were not made there. They were made for, not by, ANZAC soldiers. The biscuits did not become the "Anzac biscuits" eaten on Anzac Day until after the war, when they were baked as a way of remembering and connecting to the dead. If Australian and New Zealand women baked their national identities into being, they did so in part with the understanding that they would be Love's "anyone," that they would show up with Anzac biscuits to mitigate the effects of Anzac tiles, and of war, even small wars, like the one Love created out of professional curiosity in his kitchen.

Making and consuming Anzac biscuits as a national identity formation process underscores that as with most culturally significant foods, the Anzac biscuit becomes a metaphor for the real and imagined bodies that cook and eat it. In this sense, the Anzac biscuit functions as a reenactment. Artist and architect Kingsley Baird offers explicit collapse and conflation of biscuits, bodies, ovens and war. In addition to enduring sculptural and architectural monuments and memorials at sites around the world, Baird has created ephemeral installations that use Anzac biscuits and biscuit cutters to collapse the soldier's body with the biscuit and invite the experience of eating into the gallery. *Serve* (2010-11) presented a series of biscuit cutters inside of WWI army mess kits which have been embossed with an Anzac biscuit recipe. The biscuit cutters are sometimes missing limbs: in the below image of one of Serve kits, a leg is missing at the knee. In subsequent installations *Tomb* (2013) and *Stela* (2014), Anzac biscuits made with these cutters were offered to visitors. Baird draws attention

Lindsay Kelley

to the ways in which Anzac biscuits use historical transubstantiation to acquire their power and meaning as "culinary memorials" (Supski 2006, 52). This work suggests that all Anzac biscuits, including the plain round ones, are flesh, specifically the flesh of the dead, even more specifically the flesh of the martyred. The installations fabulate a fantasy that runs in two directions. First, this imagined historical artifact implies that soldiers in some other timeline were able to make biscuits with their mess kits (we know they were not able to bake on the battlefield, and that the bakery was only minimally competent with bread). Second, *Serve* invites bakers and eaters of Anzac biscuits to imagine their baking in new and possibly unsettling ways. Eating a gingerbread man, a chocolate rabbit, even a gummy bear, always produces a moment of humorous cannibalism as we imagine the figure's diminished capacities with each bite. With Baird's biscuits, war has already taken a bite out of them, making our subsequent bite somehow complicit with the violence of amputation. Eating an Anzac biscuit shaped like a WWI soldier conjures a war inside our mouths--our teeth explode and pulverise these crunchy men, browned under our oven sun, buried in our stomachs and the soil of our bowels.

With Baird's ephemeral memorials, we taste material connections between Australian and New Zealand national identities, soldier's bodies, and baked goods. These projects suggest that biscuit cannibalism rests on deep and shifting soils of complicity and responsibility for acts of war. Baird crafts the "memorial" part of Supski's "culinary memorial" by recalling cenotaphs, stelas, and headstones with Anzac biscuits. These works imagine a kitchen and are haunted by ovens, but *Tomb* and *Stela* do not capture the active process of making that Supski considers with her interpretation of the Anzac biscuit as a "culinary memorial". That which is culinary is "of the kitchen" or "of cookery." Anzac biscuits and fry bread are kitchen memorials. A kitchen memorial might be harder to contain than Baird's ephemeral and edible but also architectural and public installations. "Of the kitchen" means "of the home." Anzac biscuits, recalling Martha Rosler's collage series, "bring the war home." In a country where war dead were not routinely repatriated until 1966, Anzac biscuits stand in for absent bodies. Eating them reenacts imagined experiences of battle, with a sugar coating.

Recalling wheat as a state of mind in *As You Like It* and the ways in which wheat has played a part in the nutritional environment of conquest while also conquering land with the logics of monocultures, I'd like to conclude by suggesting that an anticolonial ingestion of hardtack might be possible, and that hardtack's decolonizing capacity begins with what the biscuits seem to lack: taste. Taste does not figure prominently in writing about biscuits or wheat, perhaps because its subtle flavours do not inspire description. However, blandness and seeming tastelessness are of critical importance to the wheat-based foods I describe above: this purportedly neutral palate conquered much of the world. A taste-based analysis of tastelessness holds a decolonising potential by revealing blandness to be as culturally specific and significant as that which is spicy or strong. Attending to taste encourages a deeper engagement with how wheat has been changed and engineered, and how ingestions of wheat might be at their most anticolonial when indigestion results from ingestion. Thinking about Isabelle Stenger's trouble with tolerance and the ways in which educated tolerance excuses ignorance, we might consider the increasing precarity of wheat and gluten tolerance as an environmental shift, a change in our molecular exposure, a gut clenching, bowel irritating symptom of decolonization.

Works Cited

Australian War Memorial. "Anzac biscuit recipes," accessed October 11, 2017, https://www.awm.gov.au/articles/encyclopedia/anzac/biscuit/recipe.

Australian War Memorial. "Make hard tack," accessed October 11, 2017, https://www.awm.gov.au/learn/schools/resources/hard-tack.

Detterick-Piñeda, Cynthia. (2017). "Navajo Fry Bread History," accessed October 10. http://www.snowwowl.com/recipes/recfrybreadhistory.html.

Head, Lesley, Atchison, Jennifer, and Gates, Alison. (2012). *Ingrained: A Human Bio-geography of Wheat.* New York: Routledge.

Landecker, Hannah. (2011). "Food as Exposure: Nutritional Epigenetics and the New Metabolism." *BioSocieties* 6(2), 167–194.

Love, Tony. (2016). "Hard Tacks and Bully Beef: A Critic's Harsh Review of What the Anzacs Really Ate." *The Advertiser*, accessed June 21, http://www.adelaidenow.com.au/anzac-centenary/hard-tacks-and-bully-beef-a-critics-harsh-review-of-what-the-anzacs-really-ate/news-story/3e2f5760be22b4087018b904 93d49b78.

Miller, Glenn. (2014). *Frybread: Past, Present & Future.* Seattle: CreateSpace. 86.

Miller, Jen. (2008). "Frybread: This Seemingly Simple Food is a Complicated Symbol in Navajo Culture." *Smithsonian Magazine,* accessed October 10, 2017, http://www.smithsonianmag.com/arts-culture/frybread-79191/.

Mol, Annemarie. (2008). "I Eat an Apple. On Theorizing Subjectivities." *Subjectivity* 22, 28–37.

Shakespeare, William. n.d. *As You Like It.* Champaign, Ill: Project Gutenberg, n.d. eBook Collection, accessed January 29, 2017, http://www.gutenberg.org/cache/epub/1121/pg1121-images.html.

Supski, Sian. (2006). "Anzac Biscuits: A Culinary Memorial." *Journal of Australian Studies* 30, 87.

Urban, Alan. (2017). "How to Make Hardtack: A Cracker That Lasts for Years," *Urban Survival Site*, accessed October 10, https://urbansurvivalsite.com/make-your-own-hardtack/.

Wilson, Elizabeth. (2015). *Gut Feminism.* Durham: Duke.

7   Mining Indigenous Alterity: A Critique

Eve Vincent and Timothy Neale

In a 2017 essay, we took the opportunity to pair two shared concerns of ours (Neale and Vincent 2017, 417-439).[1] On the one hand, we are interested in the political economy of the extraction of materials—namely, minerals—pulled from subterranean strata on the Australian continent. This extractive activity, often glossed as 'the Australian mining industry,' occurs on lands Indigenous peoples never ceded; lands often with Indigenous inhabitants; and, lands on which Indigenous interests are only sometimes and partially recognised by settler law. Eve's work, for example, has documented the struggles of an Indigenous group in far west South Australia who oppose the expansion of mining industry activity in their arid homeland (Vincent 2017, 26-30, 36). Other Indigenous groups in this region have entered into an agreement with a mining company through a legal process we understand as fundamentally coercive.

On the other hand, we are interested in thinking critically about the shifting moral economy surrounding Indigenous cultural difference in the academic disciplines we work across—anthropology and cultural studies. In recent decades, the potentially extractive (or, exploitative) relationship between Indigenous knowledge and scholarship has been a matter of central concern for many. The past few years, however, have seen a renewed interest in radical alterity. Encounters with 'Indigenous ontologies' have become commonplace in academic journals and conferences, as though their content and value were self-evident. Influenced by the many postcolonialist scholars who have previously suggested it was ethically suspect to look at or for alterity, we have been wondering: how and why have we now arrived at an intellectual moment that seems to accept that this difference can be both presumed, and, further, is valorised as always positive?

The longer essay on which this hack is based thus revolves around asking: What does the Australian mining industry want *with* Indigenous cultural difference? What do cultural studies, anthropology and allied disciplines each want *from* Indigenous cultural difference? In our essay, we posit these questions as interrelated and 'urgent'. They are urgent because the possibilities for being radically 'otherwise' in Australia are ever-shrinking (Povinelli 2011, 9-11, 130). In the midst of hostile conditions, what do Indigenous people want from an industry like mining? Mining might now, as some claim, be unwelcome on the basis of culturally different relations with the land and sites the extractive industry proposes to commodify. Or, engagement with mining ventures might, as others suggest, offer prospects for forms of sought-after equality. These questions are interrelated because our use of mining as an empirical case study leads us to question the extent to which the kinds of Indigenous or ontologically-alter worlds that scholars assume or seek out are extant and separate from 'us'. Are not Indigenous realities better understood as fundamentally enmeshed, in violently unequal ways, with 'our' world? Ultimately, we argue for the importance of grasping and understanding contemporary Indigenous realities. We cannot avoid or disqualify those places where Indigenous people confront, confound or disappoint in the form their lived difference takes.

• • •

Some background: Both of these areas of inquiry have witnessed somewhat of a paradigm shift over recent decades. From the 1960s onwards, broader public awareness in Australia has grown about Indigenous conceptions of 'country' as a living 'continuous entity' (Myers 1986, 60), and specific sacred sites as imbued with the ongoing presence of ancestral beings, the disturbance or destruction of which threatens their very constitution in Indigenous terms. However, in the past decade, a new story has gained ground. In *this* account, Indigenous interests are depicted as potentially commensurate with rather than obstructive of large-scale resource extraction.

The putative reconciliation of mining and Indigenous legal interests in country has been facilitated by the passage of land rights laws such as the 1993 federal native title legislation. Native title legislation, as it currently stands, provides Indigenous people with no rights to consent over what is done with their land, however most third-party land uses, such as mining, trigger opportunities to negotiate compensation or 'benefit' packages with developers. In the resulting 'native title market' these third parties are delivered security and a 'social license' to operate, while state and territory governments reap the benefits of royalties and infrastructure investments and Indigenous stakeholders are compensated via some mix of payments, employment, services and training, and so on (Ritter 2009, 27-29). Within this new era of agreement-making, Indigenous cultural difference is now valorised as a benefit to the industry, as Indigenous residents are among the few willing to stay in remote and regional areas targeted for extraction: in part, their ties to kin and country are re-appropriated as workplace benefits.[2]

Meanwhile, a shift of another kind has taken place within the academy. In the 1970s, anthropology was in crisis regarding, among other things, its historical relationship with colonialism and, more fundamentally, the idea that the discipline was reliant on making authoritative claims about so-called non-modern 'others' and extracting, or mining, their lives for insights and academic status. Anthropology's response was to foreground questions of social suffering, power, the state and so on rather than difference through the 1980s and 1990s.

Cultural studies scholars were having their own debates in this period about modes of representing otherness, though the response was quite different. If power over oppressed others was exerted through representation, then one answer was to avoid exercising further 'symbolic violence' and remain content instead to analyse representations, attentive to their particular dynamics.

As earlier mentioned, both disciplines have either turned or returned to questions of lived radical alterity, via the much-discussed 'ontological turn'. We see one important iteration of

Eve Vincent and Timothy Neale

this in the determination of some to avoid the 'modern' scission between nature and culture detailed by Latour: this has seen Indigenous 'perspectives' or 'ontologies' cited as exemplary, repositioning Indigenous cultural difference as a site of recognition and value in the Anthropocene.[3]

However, putting these two developments together leaves us with a series of questions, about which we are uneasy:

What are the politics of turning to Indigenous alterity—at the level of the abstract—in the very same moment where, in Australia and elsewhere, political developments serve—at the level of governmental interventions and the everyday—to contain, delimit, discipline and pathologise certain forms of Indigenous difference? Are these not *the* political questions that should claim our attention? Further, we question how analytically separable Indigenous or settler worlds are in a settler colonial state such as Australia. We see Indigenous lives as always enmeshed in broader material and discursive relations of power, *including discourses about the nature and value of their cultural difference.* Certain kinds of reified cultural otherness, which substantiate claims to continuity and tradition, are elicited as part of the native title claims process, for instance. Indigeneity, like the nature-culture divide, is a basic political coordinate of contemporary life, and there are considerable costs, borne by Indigenous people, associated with: being too different or not different enough; making strategic efforts to self-fashion or being too self-fashioned. We think the pertinent question is: what conditions of possibility for radical Indigenous difference actually exist? Does Indigenous involvement in extractive industry activity in remote areas, for example, serve to enable or corrode the expression and living out of Indigenous cultural difference?

We are also concerned about what happens when Indigenous people disappoint? We are arguing that 'they' might not always be as different, in an ontological sense, as what 'we' might imagine or hope 'them' to be. If it is the case that 'our' embrace of, our turning to, indigeneity is highly conditional—as we look for inspirational models of ecological wisdom and ethics—then how do we account for those Indigenous people who accept mining, who foreground their aspirations for economic equality, or who seek to revive pastoralism in degraded landscapes, for example? Is there a danger here that long-held hierarchies that devalue certain expressions of Indigeneity as compromised or corrupted, and elevate others as more 'traditional' and more culturally and analytically distinct, are recast and reinvested in through slightly new terms? What kinds of 'purifications,' to use Latourian language, are mobilised in the ontological turn?

Finally, new age spirituality has long been criticized for a superficial engagement with Indigenous culture, using it as a vehicle for self-realisation. But should we not be alert to the possibility that, again here, only *some* Indigenous people are interesting and matter to 'us' in our pursuits? And, further, that those we focus upon are those perceived to offer us the possibility of being other to ourselves, however politically necessary and urgent such an endeavor now seems in an age of environmental crisis?

We anticipate two responses to the critique we've laid out. According to the first, all of the earth's inhabitants need information on 'richer ontologies' and 'imaginative elements' to disturb our present torpor. The many Indigenous people who, through settler colonial and capitalist exploitation, find themselves today amongst the ranks of the dualist 'moderns' have no special status; they too, along with the other naturalists and analogists, must take their cue from the animists and totemists (see Descola 2013, 129–140).

According to the second, indigeneity is better understood not as essentially about primordial, transhistorical attachments, but rather as 'articulated' within contexts, comprising heterogeneous elements from here and elsewhere, now and elsewhen (Clifford 2013, 30-40). We urge scholars to proceed from an empirical basis, focused less upon broad concepts such as 'Indigenous ontology' and more upon the existence and potential arrangement of shared worlds, as they are lived within and struggled over.

Eve Vincent and Timothy Neale

Notes

1   We note that there are no universally satisfactory names for indigenous groups globally or on the Australian continent. We have used the word 'Indigenous' throughout this essay for the sake of clarity, knowing that this is nonetheless a contested term.

2   We note that anthropologist Kirk Dombrowski instructs us that Indigenous people staying behind, as well as the poverty in remote communities, is naturalised as cultural phenomena, Dombrowski 129–140.

3   For example see Latour 2002; Latour 2009, 1-2.

Works Cited

Clifford, J. (2013). *Returns: Becoming Indigenous in the Twenty-First Century*. Cambridge, MA; London, Harvard University Press.

Descola, P. (2013). *Beyond Nature and Culture*. Chicago; London, University of Chicago Press.

Dombrowski, K. (2010). "The White Hand of Capitalism and the End of Indigenism as We Know it." *The Australian Journal of Anthropology* 21, 129–140.

Latour, B. (2009). "Perspectivism: 'Type' or 'Bomb'?" *Anthropology Today* 25(2), 1–2.

Latour, B. (2002). *War of the Worlds: What about Peace?* Chicago: Prickly Paradigm Press

Myers, F. (1986). "Pintupi Country, Pintupi Self." *Sentiment, Place, and Politics among Western Desert Aborigines*. Washington and London, Smithsonian Institute.

Neale, T. and E. Vincent (2017). "Mining, Indigeneity, Alterity. Or, Mining Indigenous Alterity?" *Cultural Studies* 37(2-3), 417-439.

Povinelli, E. (2011). *Economies of Abandonment: Social Belonging and Endurance in Late Liberalism*. Durham, N.C., Duke University Press.

Ritter, D. (2009). *The Native Title Market*. Crawley, WA, UWA Press.

Vincent, E. (2017). "Against Native Title." *Conflict and Creativity in Outback Australia*. Canberra, Aboriginal Studies Press.

8   Snow Day (or, Weathering the City #1: Hacking Blizzard Infrastructure in New York City)

Jennifer Mae Hamilton

One form of the verb "hack" means "to make rough of random cuts" (hack 2018). It was once commonly used to denote frost's capacity to chap or crack the skin. This particular meaning derives from *"tōhaccian"* or to hack to pieces (hack). Bearing this violent etymology in mind, and taking New York as my muse, I ask what would it take to materially hack the Anthropocene in the archaic sense of frost cracking skin? What would it mean and what would it take for the city's lips to be seriously chapped in a snowstorm?

In asking this I reveal my melancholy and my rage. Melancholy for the melting frozen world, the disappearing permafrost, the societies, fantasies and myths built on ice. The rage comes from the relentlessness of business as usual in places like New York, and my hometown Sydney. As if this world of cars, deskwork, mortgages and disposable coffee cups is the best of all possible.

Sometimes, when a city or town receives an excess of ice and snow, a "snow day" is declared. This never happens in Sydney (occasionally we get thunder storms severe enough for political leaders to tell people to leave work early).[1] It does happen in New York. Officially, a "snow day" is when the school bus cannot make its usual route. School is cancelled, triggering a domino effect on other types of daily transportations. The city's systems stop. Beyond schooling, New York's snowstorms interrupt the capitalist flow of the iconic city by literally freezing it. The road is at the centre of this story. It is the impervious surface across which buses, cars, trucks, people, goods, services, money and capital flow. This particular kind of flow only occurs if the road can remain open and the predominantly fossil fuelled vehicles can get through. The open road belongs to business. When closed, I reckon the road promises a different kind of economy.

Janine Macleod argues that the capitalist hegemony would not function without its grab bag of watery metaphors: cash flow, the trickle down effect, currency (McLeod 57). To which I would add the flow of traffic. These watery metaphors is affected by the blockages too. When things go wrong assets are "frozen" or the roads are clogged like a drain (40). Playing with the logics of flows and freezes, my offering to Hacking the Anthropocene involves hacking into attempts to keep roads open in a snowstorm in order to find other ways to be open to the conceptually and materially disruptive logic of such weather events. This is not about openness to danger or life threatening cold. This is not to a fetishisation of the logic is not of disaster for constructing a disaster counter-capitalism, but rather a critical uptake of the dreamy news that school is cancelled because of a snow day!

After presenting my Hack to the audience at the symposium, I had two similar and similarly memorable offline responses that suggested that there is nothing dreamy about a snow day. One person said it was "cute" for an Australian to speak about the cold; where cute was equal parts patronising and refreshing. First, "cute" referred to my confident naivety, given I'd never been bogged down by the daily grind of life in the cold, living as I do in the Promised Land, Sydney. Second, "cute" also suggested that this ill-informed perspective was kind of appealing too. The second, less generous version of the same response, informed me I have no idea what I am talking about and that snow days are actually awful and make life really difficult. To paraphrase: "You really have no idea what you are talking about. You obviously haven't tried to drop the kids at school and get to work after a snowstorm." And this latter comment—an overtly patronising criticism—interests me most. This person is well-to-do. And so the intense frustration reflects an otherwise sheltered and fully-accommodated life; as such, the negative affect interests me deeply. Poorer people struggle through winter unable to change the economic structures that gives their neighbour ready access to heat, and them a drafty house and broken radiator. Meanwhile powerful and privileged frustration about the weather is performative. It shapes social norms and living standards. Why can't the more privileged amongst us just let the snow hem them in a little bit? By privileged, I mean people who have the means to keep warm and alive during and after a blizzard. I'm not saying let the poor or homeless freeze, I'm asking what else could it mean—infrastructurally, politically, ideologically, materially, emotionally—to let the snow, rather than the flow of traffic, to dominate for a day or two.

Zachary Maxwell knows what I mean when I say a snow day is dreamy, and he endures Manhattan's harsh winters. Maxwell is a young documentary maker motivated to investigate the snow day in response to a suspicion that the amount of snow days he gets per annum does not properly correspond with the abundance of snowfall he experiences. He'd prefer to stay at home and play with his little brother on a miserable and cold day, but more often than not he has to go into school. Maxwell lives on Manhattan and goes to school there too. It snows a lot on Manhattan island, but snow days are strikingly rare. He decided to investigate why he has so few snow days and discovered that there is considerable infrastructural investment to ensure that the snow day does not actually happen (Maxwell). The infrastructure is designed to keep the roads and therefore schools, businesses and stock exchanges open. It is thus not the elemental stuff of the snow itself, but the infrastructure engineered to ensure business as usual that needs attention.

In solidarity with Maxwell's youthful frustration,[2] I submit that a systematic rethinking and restructuring (a "re-infrastructuring") of the urban approach to the snow storm is a potential way to hack the Anthropocene because snow materially slows the city, troubles daily habits (school, work and consumption). We need to occupy the negative affect that builds policy in order to resist slowing along with the cold weather and from there build a new city. Wealthy cities of the global north need to be slowed down, consumption needs to change direction, the more privileged lifestyles need to be far less so, assets need to be snap frozen, human labours need to be redirected towards

Jennifer Mae Hamilton

an altogether different bottom line, how, what and why we teach is in flux too. Modern cities are icons of the extractavist age; they are materialisations of its logics. The energy intensive infrastructure that aims to keep roads open at all costs after a snowstorm is the epitome of this logic. Currently, the infrastructural investment aimed to keep roads open during a snow day represents the refusal to let the more-than-human to be anything other than ornamental in the city. The snow ploughs and salt sheds exemplify the anthropocentric logic of capitalist fossil fuelled urbanism.

I imagine the skyscrapers as inverted mines, as if all the materials extracted from the earth and the new rocks and metals synthesized—the stratigraphic matters of epoch—are represented in relief in sky, by the skyscrapers that spring up across the land as materialisations of human fantasies of transcendence.

The Spring Street Salt shed is one of 45 Salt Sheds on Manhattan Island. It is designed to look like a salt crystal and can house 5000 tonnes of salt (of the approx. 200 000 tonnes stored on Manhattan at any one time). Salt is used to clear the streets after a snowfall because the melting point of salt water is lower than fresh. On one hand, the salt shed is a green star rated building with a green roof and grey water treatment system. It is the cutting edge of sustainable design. On the other, the salt used to clear the roads is posing a range of environmental issues down stream. It is an architecturally designed paradox of urban sustainability. It is certifiably sustainable and completely unsustainable at the exact same time.

In Canada road salt is considered a toxin, but in the US the millions of tonnes of road salt used each year are causing salinization in the ground water, impacting not only human but more-than-human life. Not to mention corroding other essential infrastructures. Zachary Maxwell calculated that in one snowstorm enough salt is distributed in NYC to cover 789.5 Billion servings of medium sized fries. When discussing ecological issues around this there are currently two paths: one is to celebrate the sustainability of the salt shed in itself, despite the salt. Two is to

Figure 1. Spring Street Salt. Shed Photo by Ken Ohyama, CC-BY-SA

talk about the alternative methods of clearing the roads like beet juice or magnesium. But why not close the road? There are health and safety concerns, to be sure, the need to get some labouring women and heart-attack patients to hospital, for sure. But surely there is a standard of living healthfully and safely between the open road and the one that's clear-and-salted? Surely if labouring women and those having heart attacks took priority, while other kinds of trade in the city stopped, the snow-response team would be differently structured and Zachary Maxwell and others would get a restful snow day.

What would it mean to do freezing weather in cities differently? No one really wants to go to work when the weather is too cold, too hot or too wet, what is really lost by stopping work or school for a day or two here or there? No one likes traffic. Susan Leigh Star argued that infrastructures become visible when they fail (Star 382). What is revealed by their failure is the logic of their success. In ecological terms this weather-management infrastructure reveals the outer limit of a city's capacity to manage the force of the more-than-human world. The snow day, or what else happens during that infrastructural operation, invites thinking about changing those limits. The snow day, if it were to be thought differently, holds within it a new logic of life, learning and work in relation to weather in cities. Although I recognise there are health and safety concerns involved in having major roads through the city closed, we need to ask if essential services and servitude to capitalism can travel different roadways?

Notes

1   In a recent storm in Sydney, then state premiere Mike Baird ordered workers leave early to avoid pressure on the transport systems, because the storm was predicted for afternoon peak hour. http://www.smh.com.au/environment/weather/sydney-weather-mike-baird-calls-on-workers-to-head-home-asap-before-storm-gets-worse-20150421-1mpv4y.html

2   And others committed to rethinking infrastructure in times of environmental crisis: Stephanie LeMenager, Tess Lea, Lauren Berlant.

Works Cited

"hack, v.1." *OED Online*. Oxford University Press, January 2018. Web. 15 February 2018.

Cormack, Lucy. (2015). "Sydney weather: Mike Baird calls on workers to head home ASAP before storm gets worse," retrieved from http://www.smh.com.au/environment/weather/sydney-weather-mike-baird-calls-on-workers-to-head-home-asap-before-storm-gets-worse-20150421-1mpv4y.html

Maxwell, Zachary. *Anatomy of a Snow Day,* retrieved from *https://vimeo.com/112013365* February 15, 2018.

McLeod, Janine. (2013). "Water and the Material Imagination: Reading the Sea of Memory against the Flows of Capital" in Cecelia Chen, Janine McLeod and Astrida Neimanis, *Thinking with Water*. Montreal: McGill-Queens University Press.

Star, Susan Leigh. (1999). "The Ethnography of Infrastructure." *American Behavioral Scientist* 43.3, 382.

9   The Blind & Deaf Highway Woman

Script by Undine Sellbach and Stephen Loo

USHERs 1 and 2 [ASIDE]: We are speculative ethologists. Our method is to infest familiar sites of spectacle, adventure and learning - the picture palace, the lecture hall, the open road - with small creatures of instinct.

The audience files into the lecture hall. It is dark like a cinema. At the front there is a screen. On one side of the screen there is a glass box of buttered popcorn, on the other a lectern.

The USHERs exchange tickets for warm paper boxes of coconut water, with straws.

USHER 1:

Keep your coconut water with you, warm and close to your person.

USHER 2:

On your stomach, inside a sleeve, under your arm, in the palm of a hand, against a leg, on your lap ...

When everyone is seated [USHERs move to the lectern] the performance starts.

The words 'THE BLIND & DEAF HIGHWAY WOMAN' flicker and appear on screen.

USHER 1:

Working in the 1930's, the biologist Jakob von Uexküll proposed that animals are not machines but "machine operators."[1] Each have distinct perceptions, orientations, appetites and inner worlds, related to their specific outside environments.

USHER 2:

Uexküll's favorite example is the tick.

USHER 1:

How is a tick a machine operator?

USHER 2:

A tick, after mating, climbs up a shrub. Deaf and "eyeless" she is drawn by her photosensitive skin, and hangs on the tip of a twig, waiting for a mammal to pass beneath her.[2]

> *[USHERs 1 & 2 are silent for a few minutes]*

USHER 1:

Over this period, which may be almost her entire life span, nothing affects her.

> *The USHERs wait silently for a longer period still. Some in the Audience shift about in their seats.*

USHER 2:

The tick, smelling butyric acid, which is a chemical emitted by all mammals in their sweat, falls.

USHER 1:

Oh no!

> *The Audience, drifting off, now starts to take notice.*

USHER 2:

If she lands on a mammal, her tactile organs take over. Searching for a warm hairless spot, she bores into the mammal's skin, drinking its blood.

USHER 1:

Mmmmm. The taste of the blood is unimportant. Laboratory tests show a tick will drink from an artificial membrane containing any liquid at 37 degrees.

USHER 2:

Ladies and gentlemen, as one can see, a tick's life may be reduced to three stimuli, each anticipate an action and unfold in a particular order.

On the screen, a diagram appears. [USHER 1 demonstrates the cycle on the screen]

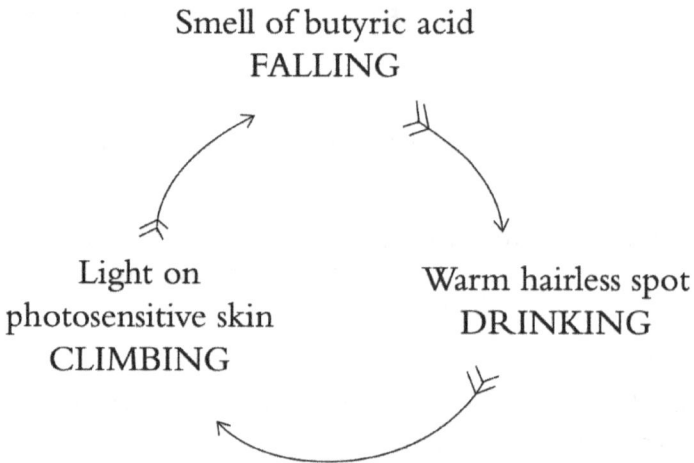

Smell of butyric acid
FALLING

Light on
photosensitive skin
CLIMBING

Warm hairless spot
DRINKING

Figure 1. Umwelt cycle of the tick.

USHER 1:

It seems that the tick's world is "constricted and transformed into an impoverished structure."[3]

USHER 2:

But for Uexküll, actively not perceiving certain stimuli, while interpreting others as significant in a distinct temporal unfolding, is precisely what distinguishes the tick as a living being from a machine.

Script by Undine Sellbach and Stephen Loo

USHER 1:

A tick actively interprets her environment, neglecting some differences, amplifying others, while a machine only reacts according to physical laws.

USHER 2:

Most famously, Uexküll imagines the tick contributing a distinct melody to a vast *symphony of nature*, where all living things are musically, but also structurally, attuned like different orchestral instruments.

USHER 1:

[USHER 2 whistles a small tune] The symphony of nature allows for the intensification of relations between all things in the environmental milieu, which Uexküll calls the *Umwelt*.

USHER 2:

What is less considered however is the improvised, playful, pantomime dimension of Uexküll's biology.

USHER 1:

The original English translation, now superseded by more neutral wording, casts the tick as a Blind and Deaf Highway Woman. Uexküll invites his readers to ventriloquize her *Umwelt*, using makeshift objects, sensations and words from their own.

USHER 2:

The tick in turn, conjures we humans as "undifferentiated" mammals.[4]

The Audience looks quizzical.

USHER 1:

The conventional scientist uses his concepts "as a means of analysis," but does not "encounter" them in real life ...[5]

USHER 2:

... but the tick meets her concepts as *living abstractions.*

> *The Audience continue to look quizzical. The USHERs get slightly worried.*

USHER 1:

Alright. To consider the strange concepts, subjects and modes of address that Uexküll's biology opens up, why don't we act out the tick's *Umwelt* cycle together!

> *The USHERs move to the front of the screen, shut their eyes and signal to the audience to follow.*

USHER 2:

The Umwelt of the tick begins with a burst of light felt by the skin. [A hot white light flashes from the screen] The feel of light on the skin signals the action: *climbing* [USHER 1 starts climbing]

> *Some Audience members, especially those clustered directly under the screen, follow - legs on chairs, arms flailing, fingers folding, lids feeling, chins reaching ...*

USHER 1:

The second affect is smell, the odour of butyric acid acts as a signal. Now, the word 'butter' is an etymological cousin of 'butyric.' Butyric acid, smells like rancid butter.

Eyeless, USHER 2 opens the box by the screen, and puts a piece of buttered popcorn in each ear. USHER 1 follows suit.

USHER 2:

As Uexküll writes: "The odour of butyric acid, acts on the tick as a signal to leave her watchtower and hurl herself downwards."[6]

> *[USHER 1 falls], while USHER 2, in a remarkable feat of unsensing, continues to move about the room, popping popcorn in*

Script by Undine Sellbach and Stephen Loo

audiences' ears. Audience members, whose organs for sound and
smell are set close together, sense the butter and start falling.

USHER 2:

[Eyes shut, ears plugged, nostrils tweaked in an effort to stay upright and distribute popcorn] As Uexküll points out, most ticks do not complete their Umwelt cycle ...

> *The room is filling with ticks, suspended between affects -*
> *waiting to feel light and start climbing, or to smell the signal*
> *for falling.*

USHER 1:

[... still falling] But if a tick is lucky, she lands on a passing mammal, and hitches a ride. [USHER 1 lands on a mammal]

USHER 2:

An artificial membrane, with liquid at 37 degrees is the signal for Boring & Drinking. [USHER 1 gropes for a box of coconut water, tucked inside his sleeve]

USHER 1:

The coconut water should now be warm and close to your person.

USHER 2:

[Falling at last, to the muffled smell of butter in her ears] On your stomach, inside a sleeve, under your arm, in the palm of a hand, against a leg, in your lap ...

USHER 1:

On finding the membrane, all a tick needs to do is operate its stinger (suitable for boring into the skin of any mammal) and drink.

USHER 2:

You need to get the straw into the drink and drink!

USHERS 1 and 2 and Audience:
[in unison] And the tick, in her sound-less, sight-less, taste-less comportment ... conjures an undifferentiated mammal.

The screen flashes, chairs topple, popcorn spoils, and straws
snap and ...

... The HIGHWAY WOMAN enters the room!

Acknowledgements

This essay was originally published in *The Creative Critic: Writing as/about Practice*, edited by Katja Hilevaara and Emily Orley (London: Routledge, 2018), 123–128.

Notes

1   Uexküll 2010, 45.

2   Uexküll 2010, 44.

3   Uexküll 2010, 51.

4   Uexküll 2010, 179.

5   Uexküll 2010, 179.

6   (Uexküll 1957, 7.

Works Cited

Uexküll, J. von. (2010). *A Foray into the Worlds of Animals and Humans with a Theory of Meaning*. Trans. by J. D. O'Neil. University of Minnesota Press, Minneapolis.

Uexküll, J. von. (1957). "A Stroll Through the Worlds of Animals and Men: A Picture Book of Invisible Worlds." In *Instinctive Behaviour: The Development of a Modern Concept*. Ed and trans. by C. H. Schiller. International Universities Press, New York.

10 On Touching Back: Learning from Objects, in and Out of Virtual Reality

Kay Are

> Is that not in the nature of touching? Is touching not by its very nature always already an involution, invitation, invisitation, wanted or unwanted, of the stranger within?
> *Karen Barad (2012, 207)*

> The desire [is] to create something that is not a complete argument... but where there are endings and beginnings all over the work. A working work.
> *Rachel Blau DuPlessis (1990, 148)*

Vacated but stink-addled pippies, dead ants, plasticky beach detritus; some fist-curled fern fronds, fragments of beer-bottle glass, fine-haired nettle heads, and a child's careful rock collection; tufts of electrocuted possum fur, weather-washed paper advertising, fingered metal waste, dirt, and other miscellaneous materials of mixed biological providence – I seal each into its envelope. Many will soon smell difficult, and the status of each as recognisably synthetic or organic will soon be hazy. I label them and arrange them within a large carton and entrust them to a postal worker.

In two days the envelopes will arrive and someone, on my behalf, will unpack them at the symposium 'Propositions for Hacking the Anthropocene' at the University of Sydney, from which place (from the registration desk? a shadowy corner table? I wasn't there) they will be distributed to delegates alongside a printed poem (see Figure 1).

The awkward miscellany and its issued directives constituted my response to the symposium's invitation to figure what it is we *don't* talk about when we talk about the Anthropocene. What sometimes dis-integrates from the dialogue, I thought then (and still do), might be its referent *per se* or, more particularly, an

//look here is an invitation   maybe you want to touch some

matter   /this is the stuff
        we write about and with,   dwell on
                                and amid   /and maybe you want
to be touched back: by bodies whose existence
                is our work's substratum, whose vanishing is
        our profound concern, and yet   whose presence to us is often
                        more talking than tangible   already gone

//what can touching do /can you feel it when
                                you are touched back   /can touching change
                our affection for matter or   what affection feels like or   could it change
the way curiosity moves (us)   /can touching back
                                amplify
                                a thing

        /curious objects   how do they ask to be
                        carried   over the course of the day   and with what   a sense
of discomfort or   or duty or   wonder and what do you do with your revolt

//okay but no need
                to carry the stranger within on your own   /it is a burden, a pleasure we share don't
        forget   /maybe your objects want to touch   each other   to be articulated
                                with the room and all its things
        how
                is your question
                                        /go on
                conjoin your objects with others   make a sculpture or sculptures but make this
        a working work,   with beginnings and endings   all over it

Figure 1.

impression of what the referent feels like; which is to say a lively, present sense of being *impressed* by the empirical matter we discuss, of feeling (in response to) its touch. What can happen differently – to a conversation; to matter; to the way we feel about either – when talk and touch are simultaneous obligations? Does carrying a thing about with us change the way we carry out our talk about it?[1]

I would now say more precisely what I wanted (and still want) was to re-integrate *attentiveness* to tactility as an open question, a working work, in the Anthropocene. Recent writing on multispeciesism (e.g., van Dooren et al. 2016) and on the entwinement of nature and capital (Moore 2016) underscores "the complex ways that we, all of us, become in consequential relationship with others" (van Dooren et al. 2016, 3). The complexity of universal unfolding is not contingent on a person's noticing it – it will not simplify or self-contain in proportion to human attention. But if 'material-discursivity' (Barad 2007) is to be taken seriously, attentiveness must be understood to bring change into effect. The act of noticing – of drawing this thing and not that other into an 'agential cut' (Barad 2007), of selecting which among all things to bring into relationship with each other and with oneself – this very act snags or colours the self-embroidering pattern, as it unfolds like an escalating Mandelbrot set. As with my installation, in this essay I want to insinuate openings for a dialogue on the role touch plays within that fractal cobecoming; a dialogue whose progress is halted by means of the intractable spaces things make for themselves, and that is concretely situated by means of the clumpy pauses between makers making things together.

Note on method

This essay's revisiting of a past event and its proposed usefulness to future applications should be read in the frame of Rachel Blau DuPlessis's supplication that we make incomplete arguments, that is, working works that can reconfigure existing structures, but which anticipate and accommodate the continual reconfiguration of the same into the future (DuPlessis 1990, 148). DuPlessis's positive appraisal of the mutability of knowledge foretold digital scholarship's affordance of the conditions for dispersed but networked collaborative revision of academic outputs: the joint construction, potentially in real time, of a fluctuating body of knowledge by means of localised contributions that do not pretend to be conclusive or inevitable. Wikipedia is a prime example of this *process*, even if it is not evidence of scholarship's intellectual rigour. But in Johanna Drucker's envisaged digital horizon, the wide, quick and more democratic dissemination of academic research that is facilitated by 'micro-units' of publishing (twitter, on-line comments, pingbacks, etc.) need not equate to a diminishing of substance: "what lies ahead is a new system of micro-contributions in the macro-scale of an extensible universe of discourse, networked, and able to be processed, searched, and assessed in ways that will augment the human peer review system [...]. In a utopian vision, a participatory scholarly environment might support multi-tiered work" (Drucker 2013). If I wish for my essay to be read as wilfully incomplete, this should also be read as an expression of hope that my scholarship become a thing literally re- and co-articulated with other makers' made *things* – with all of the agentic connotations of that word (see note 1).

This hope exists thanks to the way in which agencies such as Open Humanities Press (OHP) open works "to ongoing collaborative processes of writing, editing, updating, remixing and commenting by readers" (Living Books About Life 2017). Importantly for the themes of this chapter, OHP's Scalar Seedbooks Project realises part of the urgent work of truly engaging with objects, which may lie in resisting the temptation to tie ideas about objects down into firm conclusions, *prior* to these ideas' material circulation through platforms of dissemination and redress – a temptation copiously satisfied by the expectations that regulate academic research and publishing norms. Which is to say, part of this essay's method is to wait: for your comments, dissection, augmentation, remix and redistribution.

All the feels

Moving forward eighteen months from the symposium, and matter's intractable spaces have patterned time into a web of events depositing me at the very particular biomechanical materialisation that I now am and within which I write. Still a creative writer and maker but, by tricks of circumstance, I am also now a researcher in the scholarship of teaching and learning. Driven partly by the squeeze of the techno-imperatives of the market-mired higher education sector, partly by blue-stockinged resistance to these – and driven, too, of course, by long, historical tributaries of feminist materialist labours of thought, the stream of which I am condemned by my relatively recent birth to dip into only retrospectively, as a secondarily experienced record of unfolding events well lived and fought by others – I now pursue a curiosity, as a precisely triangulating subset of these three drives, about the practice of and the imaginary surrounding what is called, in Higher Ed, 'object-based learning' (OBL). Learning, it is said, can be magnified or motivated by students' first-hand exposure to primary materials (Hein 2009, 151): everyday objects, artefacts, specimens and artworks brought into the classroom, for instance, provide stimulus to student inquiry and the impetus for students' experimentation and problem-solving – and all of these activities are said to enable a student's construction of knowledge.[2] Having witnessed this in creative writing classrooms, I too vouch for the power of object-touch to deliver (in the words of my students) all the feels. So, that there existed an OBL discourse promised, to my newcomer mind, a literature that would think through with me my ontological questions on the role of touch in co-becoming – which is surely no more than a form of co-learning, or at least its progenitor. (Indeed, the reader is invited to read the term 'object-based learning' in this chapter as corollary to formulations of the kind 'subject/object intra-action' and 'human/more-than-human co-becoming'.)

Yet, oddly, in the educationalist literature, *feeling* objects sometimes seems to be not altogether necessary to OBL, where the implicit wager is that even only visual exposure to tactile objects, or to *another's* authoritative handling of them, can accommodate and proliferate learning modalities. Fairly accounting for this is OBL's provenance in museums' public education programs (Candlin 2010, 2). As Fiona Candlin roundly demonstrated, this history came to entwine with the ocular-centric discourses of art history to deliver us the museum as "an optical instrument" disparaging of touch, and of the touch of a non-connoisseur public in particular (Candlin 2010, 2; Meecham 2016, 66-67). Accordingly, OBL's migration to the post-secondary context has often delivered a decamped 'collections-based learning', not infrequently with an attendant prohibition on touch. This conceptualisation of OBL installs a greater chasm between it and the insights of 'somatic learning' (Matthews 1998) than would seem logical given the practical nature of OBL. Prematurely tethering OBL to museology diverts attention from evaluating the affective and pedagogical value of touch *per se*. It also delimits understanding the affective and pedagogical value of touching *profane* objects – such as the found-object miscellany of my participatory installation, as well as the diverse forms of life that feature in currently emerging narratives of multispecies studies. In collections-based learning, these existants are overlooked in favour of the kind of objects that museological and educational markets mark off as sacred.[3]

Such a reductive genealogy diminishes the immense potential I see for OBL to be framed instead as an educative practice able to bring students to deconstruct the mind-body dualism that is still a pervasive cultural myth in Western epistemologies. Significantly, this is the same mythology that Donna Haraway and others have repeatedly shown to undergird the class, sex and gender chauvanism of the Anthropocenic discourse (e.g. Haraway 2016, 49-51). In this essay, I explore the capacity of Karen Barad's interpretation of quantum field theory (QFT) to nuance the phenomenology of touch (Barad 2012, 209) in order to suggest how touch might work to stimulate learning Mattens' philosophical argument that the skin's capacity to touch in fact stems from its more primordial capacity for tactility – that is, for being touched by others (Barad 2017, 690). This capacity can explain how QFT allows us to redefine touch as reciprocity. That is, as an experience that is always a co-experience of what Anna Tsing calls a 'passionate immersion' with objects (qtd. in van Dooren et al. 2016, 5). I lastly take QFT on an excursion into virtual reality (VR), the ultimate dream scene of thought's disembodiment, where my critique of the transhumanist imaginary suggests that, counterintuitively, VR technologies represent an opportunity to approximate a deeper understanding of quantum touch and tactility. Ultimately, I suggest that VR experiences generated on 'seamful' or touch-conscious design principles (Broll and Benford 2005, 155-157) might allow us paradoxically *to instrumentalise the techno-logic of transhumanism* to prepare richer ground for our talk of (post)human responsibility to matter, which was always also human matter, in the Anthropocene.

Kay Are

Touch as immediacy, touch as handmaid, touch as timespacemattering

> We need the power of [social constructionist] theo-
> ries of how meanings and bodies get made, not in
> order to deny meanings and bodies, but in order to
> build meanings and bodies that have a chance of life.
> (Haraway 1998, 580)

Where the educational literature *does* figure touch as important to OBL, two significant tendencies (among others) emerge. First, touch's efficacy for learning is sometimes attributed to its pro-vision of pre-cognitive/emotional immediacy (Candlin 2010, 28). This is rarely explicitly argued, more commonly asserted as a casual, unexamined aspect of a broader, more critical argument (e.g., Dudley 2012, 1-3; cf. Dudley 2012, 7-8). Second, and more frequently, touch is positioned as stimulating or inciting the knowledge production which in actual terms happens elsewhere; that is, in a circumscribed mind (e.g., Hein 2009, 38; Chatterjee, Hannan and Thomson 2016, 15-18; Dudley 2012, 1; Meecham 2016, 67). Objects on this logic appear to furnish novelty focalisation devices, whereby the touching of them is construed as effec-tive and necessary only insofar as it induces (as handmaid) or inspires (as muse) the construction of knowledge within the student's enclosed, rational mind. These two notions are not peculiar to the discourse of OBL, of course. Indeed, they are cul-turally rife, and frequently embedded within significant contri-butions to scholarship that are otherwise critical and 'progres-sive'. But they are problematic insofar as they leave Cartesian mind-body distinctions untroubled. They also, therefore, leave untapped a good fifty years of feminist revisions of the epis-temological equations that fasten Woman to Body, and fasten women and their bodies to femininity, reproductive functionality and a compromised autonomy. Claims that touch teaches only by deferring the body's apparently primal reflexes into mental representations of embodied experience hitch learning to the mind's abstraction of a somatic experience. They also downplay the affectivity of objects themselves – or, indeed, of touch itself.

If the body of the thing in question is not allowed to have idio-syncratic affective – much less agentic – power to sway the student's body, viewing it behind glass is as good as touching it.

Yet, in Sandra Dudley's rich provocation, focussing instead on the materiality of the moment of sensory connection between perceiver and perceived emphasises the "evolving state of hybridity" between "the object's physical qualities and the subject's sensory modalities" and points to "the materiality of not only the object but also the subject, who experiences the world through a physical body and interprets it with a material mind" (2012 8). Indeed, there is evidence that efficient and accurate perception of an object's characteristics relies on skin contact (Klatzky and Lederman 2008, 187; Mattens 2017, 169-170). More specifically, experiments show that the hand, as the neurologi-cally exquisite locus of intentional tactile perception, continues to be central throughout a lifespan to the individual's cognitive development (Brenner and Cowle 2013, 34-35). The hand, in fact, has been pivotal to human being's evolutionary adaptation to – that is, *to the species' learning about* – our environments (Cole 2013, 4). And, for what it's worth, we know that people *like* to touch, and we know what. According to Classen's covert field study of illicit touching in museums, it is apparently rampant (Classen 2017, 2-3). Interestingly, "few objects elicit more touches than sculptured or carved hands. These almost appear to be ask-ing to be touched, especially when they are held out" (Classens 3). Something, evidentially, *compels* object-touching. What is it; what in a body does it gratify?

To be sure, Karen Barad (2012) is led, in her interpretation of the quirks of quantum field theory (QFT), to credit touch with a highly peculiar role within a quantum ontology. Touch, she avers, is not a question of one entity affecting another, as per classical cause-and-effect mechanics; rather, the event of touch *effects* a new entity. This is because, in Barad's terms, entities are not ambling about "making leaps here and there" (Barad 2012, 208). Instead, entities are continuously "making here and there from leaps" (208): the moment of entities' mutual touch,

Barad stresses, *is the invention of a particular configuration of timespacematter*.[4] Barad explains:

> Particles, fields and the void are three separate elements in classical physics, whereas they are intra-related elements in quantum field theory. [...] The vacuum [the void] is a jubilant exploration of virtuality, where virtual particles [...] are having a field day performing experiments in being and time. [...] Virtual particles [...] do not exist in space and time. They are ghostly non/existences that teeter on the edge of the infinitely fine blade between being and nonbeing (Barad 2012, 210).

The event of matter's becoming is the event of a virtual existence assuming a patch of here and now. This idea becomes clearer when we recall that moments (time) are but the fourth, inalienable dimension of material entities (space). When we say 'the moment of touch', we are saying that a bit of material existence has left virtuality to now appear on this side of the fine blade of being, because matter called on a bit of time to become its fourth dimension. Very crudely put, the emergence of entity A consists of the becoming non-virtual of a selection of particles – of, say, A_1 and A_2 – from among an infinite number of virtually existing particles. Note, though, that because these particles only emerge as A at the moment of their co-selection, and because they have never before actualised as anything, it is nonsensical to posit a before and after: there was never A_1 or A_2, until they came together as A.[5] Moreover, since touch is a sense you cannot turn off or close, your matter constantly conjoins with the matter around you, via touch. This sustained touch is responsible for continuously calling timespace out from virtuality and into being. It is not so much a question of being in constant touch with things as you move through time; more accurately, you can move through time only because you are in constant touch with things. We could say that the continuous invention of new (Actualised) material configurations produces a string of temporal increments along which matter pulls itself forward towards future becomings. Furthermore, touch promises the inexhaustibility of potential (Virtual) unions since it is at the 'hands' of touch that "an infinity of others – other beings, other spaces, other times – are aroused" (Barad 2012, 206).

Filip Mattens has noted that the long historical focus in the phenomenology of touch has been on intentional touch (Mattens 2017, 692). That is, metaphysics has sought to understand the mechanics of touch by studying the mechanics of the hand that reaches, motivated by a certain intention to perform an action on an object, such as testing its temperature, resisting its pressure or discerning its surface qualities. This approach, Mattens contends, has obscured the skin's more basic, evolutionary function as sense receptor, namely its tactility (Mattens 2017, 690). It is through varied and repeated experiences since birth of our own tactility, that is, of our ability *to be touched*, long before we have the capacity for intentional touch, that we learn the relationship between a feeling (e.g. softness) and the mechanical events that cause our feeling it (e.g. increased blanket proximity). Our cumulative "repertoire" of somatic experiences of the impact of objects on us grants us a kind of sensory empathy with which to understand and predict the sensations that objects might produce for each other (Mattens 2017, 696). Notably, in quantum mechanics, where touch is intra-action – is always the mutual conjoining of particles to materialise as a thing – touch is *always also tactility*.

What kind of learning can be occasioned by touch, where we understand touch to instantiate a material that comprises the toucher (A_1) and the touched (A_2); a thing that 'thereafter' may not be said to have existed 'hitherto'? According to QFT, touch does not merely afford unmediated access to pre-existing objects. Nor does it merely gain from (i.e. displace) an affective connection for the purposes of discrete cerebral activity. Touch broaches the seemingly unfamiliar, ontologically reorganising it so that it is/was familiar all along. And the inverse is true, too: touch opens up a re-examination of the familiar, the student 'self', revealing this self's co-implication in/as the unfamiliar. Says Barad, touching is "by its very nature always already an

Kay Are

involution, invitation, invisitation, wanted or unwanted, of the stranger within" (Barad 2012, 207). This makes salient the value of touch as a modality of *action*, whether political (Manning 2006), ethical (Grosz 1989), erotic (Freeman 2011) or educational.[6] To hazard an answer to my essay's earlier question: it may be that the experience of object-touching gratifies a body because it situates embodied experience in connection to Barad's 'stranger within'; that is, it allows students to locate within themselves an entire material-discursive history that is ontologically necessarily shared with others. And it allows them to identify themselves, in turn, as always already located within the touched object's biography (Are 2018, 8-9).

My position is that one strategy in hacking the Anthropocene from within academia and the higher-education sector may be precisely to facilitate for our students their sense of *co-location* in a material world through object-touch. This will work insofar as it can springboard students from their material embeddedness towards "[building] meanings and bodies that have a chance of life" (Haraway 1988, 580).

Touch as virtually, seamfully possible

Touch, thus, might be said to be a research methodology for the purposes of exploring and constructing an object's history that inevitably will also be an autobiography: a way of figuring the material world as it touches us back. The remainder of this essay is directed towards advocating the assumption of virtual reality as a scene within which to deploy touch as a research methodology. The purpose here is to further leverage the effects of the quantum mechanics of touch for learning. What I hope to suggest is that it is not only that QFT and VR share an idiom of virtuality, though this is not accidental. It is, furthermore, that experiencing the current stage of VR's technological development exposes one to an enhanced sense of one's own tactility – ironically, by means of the conspicuousness of VR's attempted erasure of tactility.

First, though, it is worth remarking the historical entwine-ment of the cognitive sciences with computational theory's purchase on VR, and the effect this has had on conceptualis-ing embodiment. To the minute, computer science honours an historical commitment to a "disembodied virtual sublime" that, as Caroline Bassett notes, is an imaginary that currently over-shadows competing discourses of post-representational and body-centric new media (Bassett 2015, 147n3). It should be noted that, if the term 'the imaginary' refers to "the use of narrative, pictorial or analogic structures within knowledges" Grosz et al. 1989, xix), computing is the site of the literal production of VR's narrative and pictorial structures. Elizabeth E. Wilson roundly demonstrates that the historical use of the computer as a meta-phor for the brain has contributed to narrowing "the morphol-ogy of cognition to an articulation of discrete cognitive traces inside fixed cognitive spaces" (Wilson 2016, 118). The brain-as-CPU trope, in other words, has diminished the capacity of the culture to imagine cognition as possessing a fleshy existence.[7] Philosophy, similarly, has long supported an idea of the virtual as necessarily disembodied (Grosz 2006, 77-82). While Elizabeth Grosz has a more positive take than does Wilson on the influence of the figure of the computer on the regulation of bodies (2006 86-89), I maintain that the trope is a serious concern insofar as it has safeguarded the transhumanist dream of liberation from the flesh. As Haraway observed, feminists are right to be suspi-cious of "transcendence, [since it is] a story that loses track of its mediations just where someone might be held responsible for something" (Haraway 1988, 579). Along with N Katherine Hayles, I discern the illogicality of the transhumanist imaginary where it aspires to post-subjectivity while merely expanding the preroga-tives of "the autonomous liberal subject [...] into the realm of the posthuman" (qtd. in Wolfe 2010, xv). Ubiquitous human-computer interaction enacts this contradictory logic in seeking to deliver to users a "post-digital" experience of the world that is felt as "a world that is everywhere and nowhere, in which bodies are redis-tributed through a technological economy" (Bassett 2015, 136). It may be telling – and certainly recalls OBL's ocular-centrism

Kay Are

– that the 'post-digital' contemporary experience, within which VR is a fast-developing market, self-organises around a GUI, that is, a *Graphical* User Interface, whose metaphorical language is a strongly visual language of 'windows, icons, menus and pointers' (Smyth 2015, 140).

But were feminisms to reject VR as part and parcel of a (rightful) rejection of transhumanism's specific ocular-centrism, a loss would be incurred for the thinking of touch – which, if Barad is correct, means a loss, too, for the thinking of being-as-such. Claudia Castañeda asked what feminism might learn from the touch of robots; similarly, I would ask whether the event of touch in VR can teach us something about "alternative forms of embodiment and relationality between bodies that might be useful for feminism as it seeks to challenge the making and remaking of embodied relations of inequality" (Castañeda 2001, 226).

For feminism to reap insights from the VR experience, a preliminary understanding of how 'potential' is distinct from 'possible', and the relation of both terms to 'virtual', is key here. We learn from quantum virtuality that the void's particles are not non-particles, not neatly non-existent. Rather, they have a positive existence as potential particles. Potential particles *become possible* at the point of their actualisation, that is, as they assume objective form. To understand the virtual body as a *possible* body rather than a potential body would figure it as a body that replaces the objective body. This is the transhumanist dream that one could live entirely through the body that virtual reality manufactures, the virtual body suppressing and superseding the objective body. But, *pace* transhumanism, this is not how bodies play out in virtual environments. The virtual body always remains a potential body, and potential bodies need not become possible bodies. In VR, experiences of perception and sense continue to be felt through the objective body, as though at one remove, meaning that a virtual body's objective is not to replace physical embodiment, but instead to gainfully problematize and increase the complexity of what we understand about the objective body (Carneiro de Sousa 2017, 16).

One answer, then, to the question of how VR can be useful for feminist epistemologies might lie in deploying touch as a research methodology in, for instance, creative collaborative virtual environments (CCVEs). CCVEs capitalise on the fact that "the phenomenal body [i.e. the way one *perceives* their physical, objective body in relation to the world] does not always correspond to the physical body" (Carneiro de Sousa 2017, 14). CCVEs are a mode of VR that creates "a virtual corporeality that has at the same time a phenomenological, a corporeal and a semiotic dimension" (Carneiro de Sousa 2017, 9). CCVEs furnish users with an avatar, which consists of not only a virtual body (that is, a representation of a body within the VR experience), but also a "corporeal schema", or phenomenal body – the user's "mental or internal representation" of their own physical body (Biocca qtd. in Carneiro de Sousa 2017, 14). As Pierre Lévy puts it, the "virtualisation of a given entity consists in determining the general question to which it responds, in mutating the entity in the direction of this question and redefining the initial actuality as the response to a specific question" (qtd. in Carneiro de Sousa 2017, 22). This is one example of how VR can construct a critical, comparative space in which one's corporeal schema may learn from the avatar, and adjust in response to it, without collapsing into it. Just as the void's particles jubilantly explore virtuality, experimenting with spacetime potentialities (Barad 2012, 210), so does VR offer an opportunity not to obscure the objective body but rather to deepen our understanding of it through experimentation with a multitude of potential, phenomenal bodies. Allucquére Stone, for one, has long advocated for this environment as an opportunity for exploring trans identity and embodiment (Stone 2000, 523-525). And, to be sure, such exploration is a prominent end to which VR is currently industrially and commercially put (beyond its predominant use in gaming), which includes the simulation of environments for the treatment of neurodiverse conditions (Falconer et al 2016.; Sakurai et al. 2016) and for the rehearsal of medical and design practices which are then applied to objective bodies and environments (Wade 2017; Allercamp 2013; Kacmaz Erk 2016; Smyth 2007). But this optimism

Kay Are

cannot avert the need to be on guard. There is a strong argument to be made that, predictably, the so-called metaverse was constructed to serve the same white masculinist interests that constructed the 'meat-space' universe (Stone 2000). VR's acute suspension of haptic and proprioceptive capacities may well be a result of the patriarchal priorities of the institutions driving VR's development.

At the same time, though, such suspension offers a rare thing: an experience of phenomenological (i.e. virtual, perceptual) engulfment uncoupled from an objective bodily experience of touch. This suggests VR environments to be an ideal comparative means for appreciating the particular effects, affectivity and affordances of *tactility*. Touching is not seamless in virtual environments. By design, touch in VR is a sense in absentia, yet the technology is imperfect: in the terms of design theory, this means that VR can potentially operate according to Mark Weiser's principle of 'seamfulness' (Broll and Benford 2005, 156-157). The dominant aspiration in user experience (UX) design is, conversely, "seamlessness", where the objective is to avoid drawing the user's attention to a device or material interface, since such mediation is considered an impediment to fluid interaction with and between interfaces (Broll and Benford 2005, 156). As a design principle, seamlessness is thus reminiscent of OBL discourse that frames matter as conducive to the mind's learning – material substrates are positioned as ideally invisible handmaids to, respectively, cognition and pleasurable interaction. But the flipside of this tendency is that an interface's revelation of its properties, or its seams, can be "empowering for users as it [enables] them to adapt devices to local conditions" (Cranny-Francis 2013, 33). And might not this be the very definition of 'hacking'? As Jason Moore affirms in a different context, discerning a system's points of assembly is key to the rearrangement, even dismantling, of the whole (Moore 2016, 11). VR, then, in its current, seamful stage of development, uniquely presents the "threshold conditions" that Schroeder and Rebelo describe as necessary for a user to refuse their subsumption into a technology's logic (Cranny-Francis 2013, 33). This is because the sudden

removal of touch as one of the body's tools for spatial self-loca-
tion is experienced alongside an increase in tactility, as the VR
user stumbles, trips and has their motility circumscribed by the
material space of VR use. Heightening one's awareness of the
VR interface's materiality in turn might allow the user "to position themselves more consciously, critically and creatively" in
respect of the interface (Cranny-Francis 2013, 34). Anne Cranny-
Francis invokes the epistemological benefits of isolating touch
from all human senses as object of study. Here, she is not speaking about VR – though she could be:

> If we destabilise the obviousness or naturalness of
> touch, we can locate how touch affects our everyday
> experience, including our experience of new technolo-
> gies. [...] It also enables us to explore the biopolitics of
> touch: that is, how touch [...] implicates us as embodied
> subjects in specific discourses and the values, assump-
> tions and beliefs, permissions and prohibitions that
> constitute them (Cranny-Francis 2013, 36).

If Barad is right to exhort that theorizing, as "a form of experimenting, is about being in touch" (Barad 2012, 207) – if Haraway
before her was right to condone a mode of theorising that is
"finite and dirty, not transcendent and clean" (Haraway 1997, 36)
– then scholarship is enhanced when it is led materially into the
world, or led materially to fall over or against it.

And, in equal measure, the continued development of VR technologies is enhanced by what touch can teach. This is because,
as QFT shows, embodied touch is the vehicle for the materialisation of the virtual. Being potential rather than possible
means that the virtual plane is subtended by material strata. As
we have seen in the case of CCVEs, the construction of avatars
(or potential bodies) depends on the co-existence, rather than
replacement, of objective bodies, and the phenomenal body
is empowered to learn from avatars only by virtue of the sustained distinction between its objective body and the potential body the avatar represents. When VR does not engage with
the arrangements and proclivities of its material strata, virtual

Kay Are

realities may well be prevented from becoming actual. In this sense, transhumanism's denigration of embodiment as extraneous to human being *paradoxically curtails actualisation of virtual reality's potential.* This might be a way of saying that VR technologies struggle to recognise that they exist as potential reality, preferring to figure themselves as possible reality. The transhumanist imaginary remains utopian if it fails to engage with touch; at the same time, of course, it becomes incoherent as soon as it accepts that embodiment is a vital hinge on experience. Thus, two fates present themselves to VR. First is the possibility of reiterating a disembodied spectacle endlessly into the future, in which scenario, of course, innovation in technology, products and services will still occur, though development beyond the self-defeating bind of the transhumanist imaginary will not. If, however, VR is used as a platform for exploring and learning from the phenomenology of touch, it is more likely that VR *actualises* as an entry point into a metaverse that would not be an alternative to the universe, but rather a field of potential universes accessible to embodied experimentation.

Thus, the distance between VR and QFT turns out to be something more like a queer proximity. Despite VR's dream of immateriality and QFT's faith in matter as mattering, both engender an imaginative force that, as Barad says, quoting Kathyrn Yussoff, "puts us in touch with the possibilities for sensing the insensible, the indeterminate, 'that which travels along the edge of being, [that] is not being, but the opening of being toward' the other" (Barad 2012, 216). QFT achieves *with* matter that which VR will fail to achieve without it.

Conclusion

Can we risk granting that discourse is so many material ways of being-in-the-world, *and* that being-in-the-world means being always physically, particulately, imbricated with each other each? Worrying these questions has recently been part of the project of the material turn, the affective turn, the ontological turn, concretely; but, also, the sensory, posthuman, animal and anthropocenic turns, and the postcolonial turn before all these.[8] These movements have *together* turned to parsing points of phenomenological contact between species, between subjects, between subjects and objects. But, more than this, these movements (caught up, as they are, in the taillights of deconstruction) have consistently sought to reclaim such contact zones as evidence of the ontological illegitimacy of distinction-making practices in the first place. We have never been modern, never other than naturecultures; never less than more-than-human, and always mind and matter, both. And always cyborg, more or less, from the beginning. As a site of immersion, the participatory installation this chapter began by reporting on sought to construct contact zones in which to simultaneously carry materials and carry on a conversation, in recognition that matter and discourse are differing modalities of the one reality. QFT provides tools for thinking the immersive experience of virtual unions. Notably, Barad arrives at her interpretation of QFT by drawing on scientific-positivist and constructionist ontologies alike: her approach is diffractive; fittingly conciliatory. In light of the 'Anthropocene' and the troubling binaries that undergird our talk about it (Crist 2013, passim), this might be what we are most in need of now: not for one concept to replace another, not an either/or, but rather for an altogether queerer conceptual imaginary that is able to imagine what it means, and how, to be both.

Acknowledgements

The author thanks Oliver Rozynski, polymath and autodidact VR philosopher-designer, and profoundly loved brother, for the many VR conversations and prototyping, and, in particular, for having inspired this paper with his observation that 'cultures are virtual realities made of language'. This essay is dedicated to his forever virtual timespacemattering.

Notes

1   For the sakes of simplicity and accessibility to an interdisciplinary audience, this essay uses 'object', 'thing' and 'entity'

without discrimination – though the agential flavor of 'thing' (Bennett xvi-xvii) does foreshadow my argument here, which favours what might be called a kind of 'thing-based learning' over and above what is known as 'object-based learning'.

2   This sentence grossly condenses theories originating with the heavyweights of behavioural and developmental psychology and educational philosophy, such as Dewey, Piaget, Vygotsky and Kolb. Such theories and the progressive build of their tenets is nicely encapsulated in Chatterjee, Hannan & Thompson (2016, 12-16).

3   For a comprehensive inventory see van Dooren, Thom, Eden Kirksey and Ursula Münster. "Multispecies Studies: Cultivating Arts of Attentiveness." *Environmental Humanities* 8(1) (2016): 1-23.

4   Or, the invention of a 'cut'; see Barad (2007), 217.

5   I am relying here on 'before' and 'after', a Newtownian concept of sequential time, because it is rhetorically useful; indeed, impossible to avoid in written English. See Barad (2007), 139-140, on the kooky temporalities of intra-action. Also see Rozynski (2015) on what this kookiness can mean for writing practice.

6   All of which are arguably always manifestations of the political, anyway. Manning (2006) and Grosz (2017) speak, but differently from each other and not in the terms of QFT, of touch and bodies as offering a kind of pure potentiality that in itself constitutes the possibility of a politics or an ethics. Diffracting these positions through the ideas on touch presented in this essay is my project's future task.

7   But also see Castañeda (2001) on the reverse direction of influence between culture and technology, for instance in the way potential in the development of robotic life is circumscribed by an apparent drive to have robots emulate the model of the (male) human.

8   Though, in the context of what we learn from particulate imbrication and QFT's nonlinear time, such a dialectical conception of scholarship as iteratively 'turning' makes little sense. See van der Tuin's argument on why the 'materialist turn' might profitably lead to a rejection *tout court* of the either/or sequencing proper to the scholarly 'turn' (272).

Works Cited

Allercamp, Dennis. (2013). *Tactile Perception of Textiles in a Virtual-Reality System*. Berlin: Springer.

Are, Kay. (2018). "Touching Stories: Objects, Writing, Diffraction and the Ethical hazard of Self-Reflexivity." *Text: Journal of Writing and Writing Courses* 48: Special Issue "Climates of Change" (October), n.p., http://www.textjournal.com.au/speciss/issue51/Are.pdf

Barad, Karen M. (2007). *Meeting the Universe Halfway: Quantum Physics and the Entanglement of Matter and Meaning*. Durham, N.C: Duke University Press.

Barad, Karen M. (2012). "On Touching: The Inhuman That Therefore I Am.' *differences* 25(3), 206-223,retrieved from https://doi.org/10.1215/10407391-1892943.

Bassett, Caroline. (2015). "Not Now? Feminism, Technology, Postdigital." In *Postdigital Aesthetics: Art, Computation and Design*, edited by David Berry and Michael Dieter. Houndsmills: Palgrave Macmillan. 136-149.

Bennett, Jane. (2010). *Vibrant Matter: A Political Ecology of Things*. Durham, N.C: Duke University Press.

Brenner, A. J. and D. Cowle. (2013). "Developmental Origins of the Hand in the Mind, and the Role of the Hand in the Development of the Mind." In *The Hand, an Organ of the Mind: What the Manual Tells the Mental*, edited by Zdravco Radman. Cambridge, Mass.: The MIT Press. 27-55.

Broll, G. and S Benford. (2005). "Seamful Design for Location-Based Mobile Games." In Kishino F., Kitamura Y., Kato H., Nagata N (eds.) *Entertainment Computing – ICEC 2005*. ICEC :155-166, retrieved from https://doi-org.ezp.lib.unimelb.edu.au/10.1007/11558651_16.

Candlin, Fiona. (2010). *Art, Museums and Touch*. Manchester: Manchester University Press.

Carneiro de Sousa, Catarina. (2017). "Virtual Corporeality and Aesthetic Experience." *Virtual Creativity* 7(1), 7-28, retrieved from https://doi.org/10.1386/vcr.7.1.7_1.

Castañeda, Claudia. (2001). "Robotic Skin: The Future of Touch?" In *Thinking Through the Skin*, edited by Sara Ahmed and Jackie Stacey. London and New York: Routledge. 223-236.

Chatterjee, Helen, Leonie Hannan and Linda Thomson. (2016). "An Introduction to Object-Based Learning and Multisensory Engagement." In *Engaging the Senses: Object-Based Learning in Higher Education*, edited by Helen Chatterjee and Leonie Hannan, 13-29. New York: Routledge (eBook).

Classen, Constance. (2017). *The Museum of the Senses: Experiencing Art and Collections*. London: Bloomsbury.

Cole J. (2013). "'Capable of Whatever Man's Ingenuity Suggests': Agency, Deafferentation, and the Control of Movement." *The Hand, an Organ of the Mind: What the Manual Tells the Mental*. Edited by Zdravco Radman. Cambridge, Mass.: The MIT Press. 3-25.

Cranny-Francis, Anne. (2013). *Technology and Touch: The Biopolitics of Emerging Technologies*. Basingstoke: Palgrave Macmillan.

Crist, Eileen. (2013). "On the Poverty of our Nomenclature." *Environmental Humanities* 3(1),129-147, retrieved from https://doi.org/10.1215/22011919-3611266.

Drucker, Johanna. (2013). "Scholarly Publishing: Micro Units and the Macro Scale'. *Amodern* 1(1) (February), retrieved from http://amodern.net/article/scholarly-publishing-micro-units-and-the-macro-scale/ Accessed on 9 October 2018.

Dudley, Sandra H. (2012). "Encountering a Chinese Horse: Engaging With the Thingness of Things." In *Museum Objects: Experiencing the Properties of Things*, edited by Sandra H. Dudley. London and New York: Routledge. 1-15.

duPlessis, Rachel Blau. (1990). *The Pink Guitar: Writing as Feminist Practice*. New York: Routledge.

Falconer, Caroline J., Aitor Rovira, John A. King, Paul Gilbert, Angus Antley, Pasco Fearon, Neil Ralph, Mel Slater and Chris Brewin. (2016). "Embodying Self-Compassion Within Virtual Reality and its Effects on Patients With Depression." *BJPsych Open* 2(1), 74-80, retrieved from https://doi.org/10.1192/bjpo.bp.115.002147.

Freeman, Elizabeth. (2011). *Time Binds: Queer Temporalities, Queer Histories*. North Carolina: Duke University Press.

Grosz, Elizabeth A. (2017). *The Incorporeal: Ontology, Ethics, and the Limits of Materialism*. New York: Columbia University Press.

Grosz, Elisabeth A. and Peter Eisenman. (2006). *Architecture from the Outside: Essays on Virtual and Real Space*. Cambridge, Mass: The MIT Press.

Grosz, Elisabeth A., Julia Kristeva, Luce Irigaray and Michele Le Doeuff. (1989). *Sexual Subversions: Three French Feminists*. Sydney: Allen & Unwin.

Haraway, Donna. (1988). "Situated Knowledges: The Science Question in Feminism and the Privilege of Partial Perspective." Feminist Studies 14(3) (Autumn), 575-599, retrieved from https://doi.org/10.2307/3178066.

Haraway, Donna. (1991). *Simians, Cyborgs, and Women: The Reinvention of Nature*. New York: Routledge.

Haraway, Donna. (1997). *Modest_Witness@Second_Millenium. FemaleMan©_Meets_OncoMouse™: Feminism and Technoscience*. New York: Routledge.

Haraway, Donna. (2016). *Staying with the Trouble: Making Kin in the Chthulucene*. Durham, N. C: Durham University Press.

Hein, George E. (2009). *Learning in the Museum*. 2nd ed. London: Routledge, .

Kacmaz Erk, Gul. (2016). "Living in the Matrix: Virtual Reality Systems and Hyperspatial Representation in Architecture." *The International Journal of New Media, Technology and the Arts* 11(4), 13-25, https://doi.org/10.18848/2326-9987/cgp/v11i04/13-25.

Klatzky, R. and Lederman, S. J. (2008). "Object Recognition by Touch." *Blindness and Brain Plasticity in Navigation and Object Perception*. Edited by John J. Riener, Daniel H. Ashmead, Ford F. Ebner and Anne L. Corn, 185-207. New York: Lawrence Erlbaum Associates.

Manning, Erin. (2006). *Politics of Touch: Sense, Movement, Sovereignty*. Minneapolis: University of Minnesota Press.

Mattens, Filip. (2017). "The Sense of Touch: From Tactility to Tactual Probing." *Australasian Journal of Philosophy* 95(4), 688-701, retrieved from https://doi.org/10.1080/00048402.2016.1263870.

Matthews, Jonathan C. (1998). "Somatic Knowing and Education."
The Educational Forum 62(3), 236-242, retrieved from https://doi.
org/10.1080/00131729808984349.

Meecham, P. (2016). "Talking About Things: Internationalisation of
the Curriculum Through Object-Based Learning." In *Engaging
the Senses: Object-Based Learning in Higher Education* edited
by Helen Chatterjee and Leonie Hannan, 66-81. New York:
Routledge. (eBook).

Moore, Jason W. (2016). "Anthropocene or Capitalocene? Nature,
History, and the Crisis of Capitalism." In *Anthropocene or
Capitalocene? Nature, History, and the Crisis of Capitalism*, edited
by Jason W. Moore, 1-11. Oakland, CA: PM Press/Kairos.

Open Humanities Press. (2017). "Living Books About Life". Accessed
18 October. http://www.openhumanitiespress.org/labs/
living-books-about-life/.

Rozynski, Kay. (2017). "Assembling Bodies: A New Materialist
Approach to Writing Practice." *Axon: Creative Explorations* 5(2)
http://www.axonjournal.com.au/issue-9/assembling-bodies.
Accessed 1 December.

Sakurai, Sho, Takuji Narumi, Tomohiro Tanikawa and Michitaka
Hirose. (2016). "Making Emotion and Decision via Affecting
Self-Perception.' *Emotional Engineering* 4, 165-187, https://doi.
org/10.1007/978-3-319-29433-9_9.

Smyth, Michael. (2007). "Designing for Embodied Interaction:
Experiencing Artefacts With and Through the Body." In *The
State of the Real: Aesthetics in the Digital Age*, edited by Damian
Sutton, Susan Brind and Ray McKenzie, 140-150. London and New
York: I. B. Tauris.

Stone, Roseanne Allucquére. (2000). "Will the Real Body Please
Stand Up? Boundary Stories About Virtual Cultures." In *The
Cybercultures Reader*, edited by David Bell and Barbara M
Kennedy, 504-528. London and New York: Routledge.

van der Tuin, Iris. (2011). "New Feminist Materialisms (Review
Essay)." *Women's Studies International Forum* 34(4) (July): 271-277,
retrieved from https://doi.org/10.1016/j.wsif.2011.04.002.

van Dooren, Thom, Eden Kirksey and Ursula Münster. (2016). "Multispecies Studies: Cultivating Arts of Attentiveness." *Environmental Humanities* 8(1), 1-23, retrieved from https://doi.org/10.1215/22011919-3527695.

Wade, Andrew. (2017). "Revolution in Touch." *The Engineer*. Sept, 22-24.

Wilson, Elizabeth A. (2016). *Neural Geographies: Feminism and the Microstructure of Cognition*. 2nd ed. Abingdon: Routledge.

Wolfe, Cary. (2010). *What Is Posthumanism?* Minneapolis: University of Minnesota Press.

11 Kathy As Bowie (2015)

Kathy High

Dear David Bowie,

I have a bargain for you... I am writing you with a strange request... I am a life-long fan...

I have been following your career since I was little. I was born in 1954, so not that much younger than you... but enough so that I feel like a younger sister.

I offer these photos to you — re-enacting famous images of your career. I know thousands of fans have done the same — Tilda, probably the best, but I humbly offer mine among the others.

I was hoping these photos might capture your attention for a moment.

I want to exchange these for a throw-away item. Your poo.

I want to conduct a fecal transplantation with your stool — implanting your poop/gut biome into my colon.

This goes against all the "rules" — it should be someone close to me, someone under 60, pre-tested, etc., but I know we will be compatible.

And basically if I could become you...well, say no more...

I know people, who know people, who know people, who can probably get this letter into your hands.

I hope you will look upon this strange request favorably. I have Crohn's disease and you could change my life forever — although you already have!

I eagerly await your response.

Your fan,

Kathy

Kathy

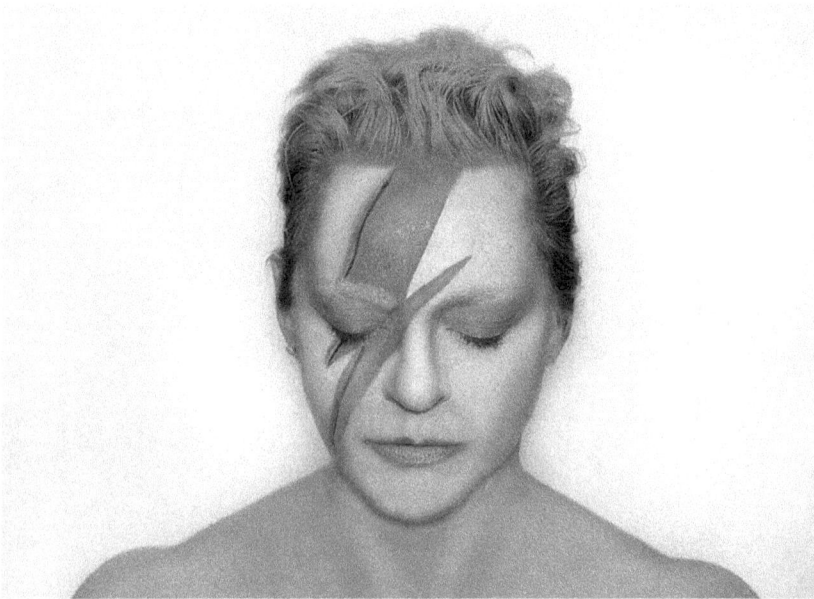

"Kathy As Bowie" is a performative piece about taking on someone else's identity through sharing their gut microbiome via a FMT/fecal microbial transplantation. Photographs were offered to David Bowie in exchange for a poop sample. The offer was never completed as Bowie died in 2016. Looking at research in fecal microbial transplants and gut microbiomes to better understand the important function of bacteria in our bodies, this project embraces metaphors of interspecies love. As a patient with Crohn's disease, High's interest in gut microbiota starts with her own body.

Kathy High

Kathy As Bowie (2015)

Kathy High

Photographer: Eleanor Goldsmith

12 Termitaria

Perdita Phillips

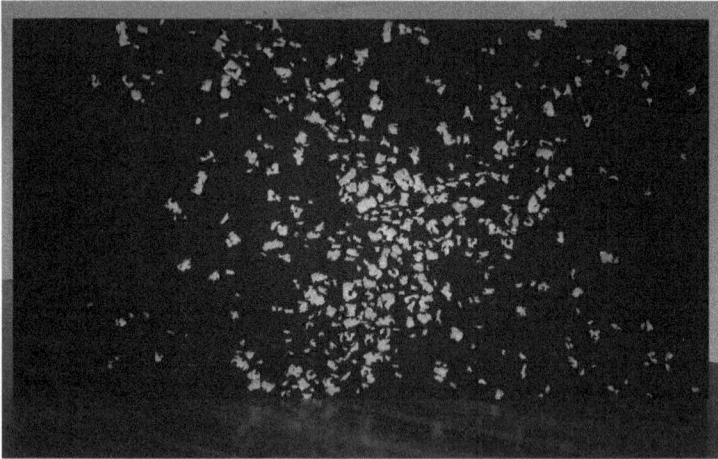

Tender Leavings (2016/2018) by Perdita Phillips. Detail of mixed media installation in collaboration with termites (850 romance novels buried for one year in a desert sand dune). Photo © Perdita Phillips.

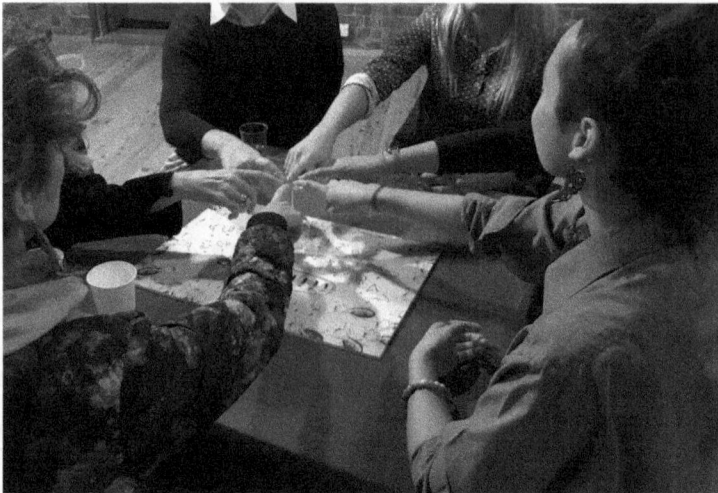

Caution, workers below (termite ouija board) (2016) by Perdita Phillips-Documentation of performative sculpture (print on paper, wine glass, furniture). Photo © Perdita Phillips.

Part 2: Hacking The Anthropocene 2: Weathering (2017)

13 Weathering in Common: Disaggregation in Stone and Humans

Denis Byrne

The seawall

During the summer of 1980 I often lay sunbathing on the lawn of Beare Park at Elizabeth Bay. The park was created when the inner reaches of this bay on Sydney Harbour were reclaimed in the 1880s by constructing a stone wall and infilling the space behind it. But in 1980, lacking any clear understanding that I was lying on a reclamation, I had no inkling that below me, down through several meters of infill, lay a remnant beach. No echo of the waves that a century ago had run up the sand of that beach reached my ear where it rested on the grass.

After a year living at Elizabeth Bay, in 1981 I moved on to a series of rental addresses elsewhere in the city, hardly ever returning. But in 2015 I began revisiting Beare Park and became newly involved with the reclamation and particularly with the

Figure 1. Pre-WW II aerial view with Elizabeth Bay at the left and Rush-cutters Bay centre (City of Sydney Archives). The photograph is assumed to date from the early 1940s. Photographer unknown.

sandstone seawall that contains the park and protects it from the harbour waters. The story I want to tell now is partly about how this wall gave me the chance to explore my geosubjectivity. Kathryn Yusoff observes that,

> As human history gives way to geologic horizons, the matter of human subjectivity must change and reach beyond life and the organism to think its way through the stratified layers of the earth's formation. It must abandon its anthropogenesis – in order, ironically, that it can say something about how to live beyond the material erasure of the Holocene (Yusoff 2016, 22).

The organisers of this symposium have called on us to respond to the question: "what are we expected to weather in the time of the Anthropocene"? Material erasure seems to offer part of the answer.

Cruising the waterline

When the sea level rose more than 120 metres following the end of the last glaciation, a relatively steep-sided river valley on the east coast of Australia was inundated and Sydney Harbour took shape. Reaching its present level about 2000 years ago, the harbour, with its convoluted shoreline, occupied fifty-five square kilometres. In January 1788, the British arrived, sailing in between the spectacular sandstone cliffs that mark the harbour's entrance. A century later the seawall at Elizabeth Bay was constructed. In the time in between those two events, the Gadigal, the Aboriginal clan whose estate included the area of Elizabeth Bay, weathered the white invasion. Some of those who survived the introduced disease, probably smallpox, that ravaged their population in 1789, dwelt briefly at a "village" of huts built for them at Elizabeth Bay by Governor Macquarie in 1820, the remains of which may lie under Beare Park. Subsequently they camped around the corner at Rushcutters Bay.[1]

The 1880s act of reclamation involved building a curved sandstone seawall across the intertidal zone of the embayment and then infilling the space behind with waste material and very

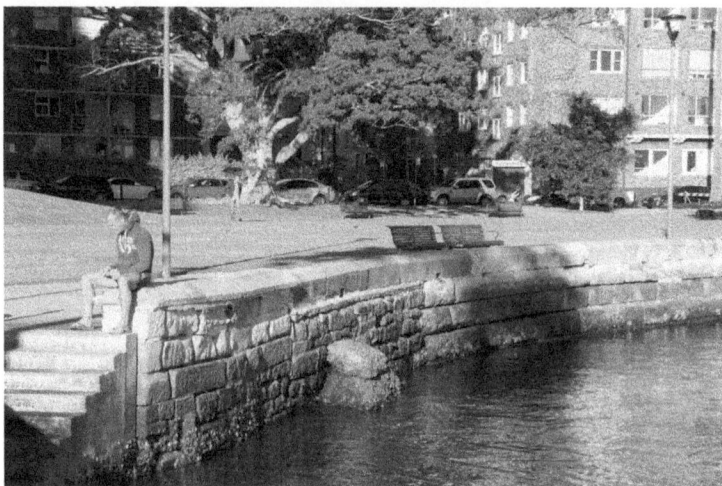

Figure 2. The Elizabeth Bay sea wall and reclamation from the east. (Denis Byrne 2015)

likely with sediment dredged from the near-shore bed of the harbour. Similar reclamations had been carried out elsewhere around the harbour's middle and inner reaches during the nineteenth century to create port facilities and make space for foreshore parks. Sydneysiders think of the harbour as their greatest natural asset but it might better be described, after Latour, as an "imbroglio" of human and more than human intensities.

The Elizabeth Bay seawall was built of large blocks of Hawkesbury Sandstone. This is a sedimentary rock formed during the Triassic Period between 200 and 400 million years ago. Sand that had washed down a river system from far inland had been deposited to form a floodplain in the present-day Sydney region and over millions of years this sand compacted to form the sandstone that is Sydney's bedrock. Extensively quarried from the 1780s, the yellow-brown rock was used in the construction of houses and public buildings, curb stones, walls and bridges.

I tended to think of the wall as a static barrier to the sea until one afternoon in 2015 I stood at low tide on the narrow strip of beach at the foot of the wall and saw how quickly the stone blocks were eroding. Although Hawkesbury sandstone has great compressive strength it erodes relatively quickly in a process

Denis Byrne

Figure 3. Elizabeth Bay seawall with the harbour beyond.
(Denis Byrne 2016)

of "disaggregation" in which the clays and other minerals that bind together the silica grains in the stone dissolve, leaving the affected grains of sand to fall away. At Elizabeth Bay, disaggregation is aggravated by soluble airborne salts from the harbour which penetrate the sandstone and crystallise there. What should have always been obvious to me was that the quartz grains falling from the eroding sandstone were not just accumulating on the beach; they *were* the beach, which is to say they assimilated into the mix of quartz grains already there. The quartz grains that ended up in the stone after having washed downriver during the Triassic were now washing around in another kind of water, the harbour water that the wall was built to defend against. The sandstone blocks that were level with my eyes as I stood on the beach were giving up their substance rapidly, on a geological timescale, but too slowly for we visitors to the park to ordinarily notice.

Witnessing the sandstone's erosion up close, I experienced a small inner lurch as the Cartesian separation of my own being from the sandstone's being gave way. I am at an age at which I can claim a certain amount of duration (I have persisted through time) and I can readily see the effects of weathering, erosion, and wear and tear on my body. This weathering has left marks on me that show where I have been. These marks are traces, in an archaeological sense. Like the sandstone, I am disaggregating, and perhaps it is that which creates the conditions for me to feel an affinity for the stone. The mundane fact of my unravelling confronts me every morning in the bathroom mirror, a vision that is at once bemusing and unfathomable (I say "unfathomable", though somewhere a not-dispassionate archaeologist's eye is observing, measuring, calibrating).

Meanwhile down at the seawall, what that little lurch *feels* like is not a shudder of mortality passing through me but a lurch of recognition, recognition that while the thingness and temporality of the stone are vastly different to my own, in terms of decay the difference is not incommensurable. In this particular case, at least, the affects of decay become a vector of connectivity between the human and the more-than-human.

We might think of reclamations as constituting a materialization, almost a monumentalization, of the culture-nature binary. The ecologically rich ecotonal transition zone between aquatic and terrestrial ecosystems is erased in favour of what seems a hard interface between land and sea. This may lead us to see reclamations as an attack on nature, but as Karen Barad reminds us,

> [...] in an important sense, there are no 'acts against nature', not if they entail the sense of absolute exteriority that is usually assumed [...] there is no outside of nature from which to act; there are only 'acts of nature' (Barad 2012, 47).

Seen from this angle, reclamations are no more "against nature" than the queer cruising that occurs in the park, especially after sundown. The cruisers and the reclamation's 'nature' interfold: desiring bodies reach for the amenity of the reclamation's space and are enfolded in a sensorium of water sounds, salt air, the rustle of leaves, the prickling of grass against skin.

Becoming intimate with the seawall on that afternoon in 2015, and on later visits, involved me in memories of cruising in the early 1980s. Mathew Gandy, in his essay on the queer ecology of

Denis Byrne

Figure 4. A section of the seawall showing severe erosion of some of the sandstone blocks. The top of the wall in the foreground was capped with concrete mortar several decades ago, subsequent to which the sandstone tier directly below has continued to erode landwards (Denis Byrne 2016)

a North London cemetery, says that "If cruising is understood as a complex interplay between bodies and space then a queer reading of space reveals a distributed agency of desire that extends beyond individuals or even multiple human bodies to incorporate nonhuman nature, inanimate objects, surfaces and smells" (Gandy 2012, 738). At Elizabeth Bay it extended to include the seawall as an agentic entity that, as we have seen, not only extends its affects and substance seaward but also landward to engage the bodies of those who lean against it, sit on it, or, to invoke a watery metaphor, cruise along it.

Mathew Gandy also draws our attention to the way that the *time* of cruising and public sex tends very much to be the time of the here and now: "The sense of stilled time experienced through encounters with gardens, cemeteries, or nature itself links with modes of sensory experience that heighten not only the experience of the present but also an existential awareness of human finitude" (Gandy 2012, 733). This idea of "stilled time" resonates with my experience of witnessing the sandstone's erosion 'up close and personal' in 2015. Simultaneous with what I've described as a lurch of recognition there was something akin to a sigh of relief that might have been a sigh of release. Given the enormous and sustained bodily effort we devote to keeping the Cartesian human-nonhuman dualism in place, it is hardly surprising that a sigh should accompany the moment when it temporarily gives way (as I stand on the narrow beach gazing at the wall, behind me the sea gathers itself to run up the sand then fall back again with a sigh). My own sigh is inflected with regret at the years of life that fill the space between what are for me rare moments of real intimacy with the world. I am deflated at this, but mostly I am caught in the "rare moment", falling into the cavity of stilled time.

Sarah Ensor suggests a link between the ephemeral "impersonal intimacies" of cruising, which she conceives as entailing an "impersonal lessness" (less duration, say, than long-term sexual relationships) and an environmentalism where "being less" might help us "loosen our proprietary claims to autonomous subjectivity" (Ensor 2017, 158). These days being less is okay. In fact, being less may be crucial to those moments when we open ourselves to things. So, in my case, perhaps it was not just an awareness of physical diminishment, via aging and decay, that brought me closer to the sandstone. A lessening of my subjectivity as human, with all the implications of hierarchical superiority to stone which that carries, removed an obstacle to engaging with it and realising that we have weathering in common.

Rhythms of aggregation and disaggregation

Back again at the seawall I am watching grains of sand fall from the sandstone blocks. As the blocks lose mass the watery space of the harbour increases minutely and the terrestrial space of the reclamation shrinks minutely. The wall's erosion allows the sea to advance inland a millimetre at a time. If we concede that the waves hitting the wall intend not to end there but to run up the sandy surface of the former beach, just as they did in the

Denis Byrne

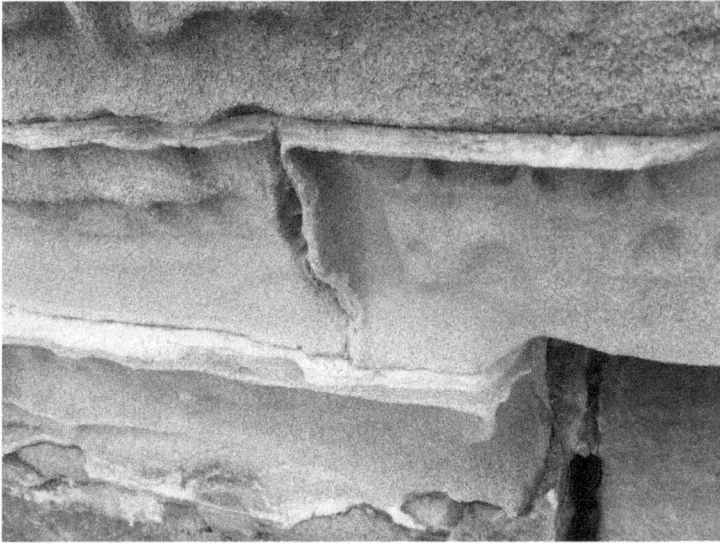

Figure 5. Sandstone blocks shown 'withdrawing', via erosion, from the cement mortar (Denis Byrne 2015).

days before the wall was built, then it follows, to my mind, that the eroding wall is responding to the sea's intentions as much as it is to our intention that the wall keep the sea out of the reclamation.

At Elizabeth Bay, from what I can see, the sandstone has formed an alliance with the sea which deals a blow to our plans for the seawall. In eroding, the sandstone blocks shrug off the rectangular dressing given to them by the 19th century quarrymen and take on the sinuous shapes congenial to their own matter and to their characteristic mode of decay. These curvaceous forms suggest the metaphor of the fold in Merleau-Ponty's (1968) phenomenology and Deleuze's (1993) work on folded matter. The kneading/folding metaphor has a key role in Michel Serres' account of non-linear time and history, an account in which events from different eras bend towards each other, becoming adjacent or coexistent, evoking the figure of a "crumpled handkerchief" (Serres 1997, 60). For Steven Connor, this gives us as an image "not of time moving on and dissipating, but of it endlessly regathering itself" (Connor n.d., n.p.). I think of the small harbour waves that regather themselves to break once more against the seawall and of how my own history involves a gathering and regathering at this reclamation across more than 30 years. The history of this place is a matter of rhythms and repetitions rather than linear progression. Included here, of course, are the rhythmic movements of the waterline in response to diurnal and monthly tide cycles, and the rhythm of the spring and neap tide cycle, but also the much more stretched-out rhythm of the glacial and interglacial cycle of the Quaternary Period we were born into.

Reclamations expand humanity's terrestrial foothold out into the sea but the displaced sea constantly worries the edges of the reclamation, testing its resolve.[2] Waves lap and slap against the stone or concrete surfaces of seawalls, swells heave against them. In a rhythm that emulates the glacial-interglacial cycle, anthropogenic sea level rise threatens to reclaim the space of the reclamation. The terrestrial authorities will of course push back against this "move" – I can see the Elizabeth Bay seawall being raised a metre, then another metre – but this has implications for the amenity of human life on the shore. Who wants a seawall that you can't see over? The play of water against the reclamation is just the thin end of a force of planetary proportions captured in the often-forgotten fact that seventy percent of the Earth's surface is sea. But the drama at the reclamation waterline is not to be reduced to a pressing of 'nature' (the sea) against the human (the seawall), since whether they are stone or concrete, these walls are themselves geological phenomena.

My relationship with the top of the wall at Elizabeth Bay is actually more intimate than with its seaward face. When I sit on the wall or stand against it, my hands absent-mindedly touch and caress its surface and come away with grains of sand attached. Some of these end up in my pockets so that I become an unwitting agent of the wall's further dispersion. At some point in the wall's 130-year history, iron pegs to support a low railing were sunk into holes drilled vertically into the sandstone blocks of the wall's parapet and were cemented in place with mortar. The railings had been removed by the time I arrived on the scene in 1980, but the stumps of the iron pegs would have been there, just as they are now, evenly spaced along the top of the wall. Some

Denis Byrne

have rusted badly in the salt air and the sea spray that drifts over the wall in heavy weather. In the process of oxidizing, the iron has expanded, exerting enough pressure to crack the surrounding sandstone, much the way that in other climates water seeps into cracks in rocks and then splits them when it freezes. The iron's propensity to rust has perhaps damaged the wall in its role as a "hard defence." The small wave of anger I experienced when I first noticed the cracking of the rock was not to do with the undermining of a hard defense but with the damage caused to something I am fond of by the callous indifference or lack of forethought of those who penetrated the stone with rust-prone iron. There is a strangeness in their not allowing for the certainty of rust occurring. Does it speak to a difficulty with the notion that an artefact of ours (the iron peg) could, without our consent, damage another of our artefacts (the wall), to say nothing of a scenario in which the iron, the salt and the stone form an alliance to the same end.

Sunset

If, for argument's sake, we take 1945 as the Holocene's end point, then clearly by 1980 I was living well inside the Anthropocene. However, the Holocene lingered on as a state of mind long after 1945 and I now wonder whether the golden tinge, which when I look back seemed to suffuse my life in 1980, owed something to the long drawn out Holocene sunset. I now see that as I lay on the summer lawn at Elizabeth Bay in 1980 I was living in what Cymene Howe has called, the "halcyon days of the Holocene" (Howe 2016, n.p.) Living in the Anthropocene, our lives are shaped, though not determined, by the material products left behind by a humanity that has hugely magnified its capacity to produce material products. Reclamations are products that have proliferated since 1945 but it is not helpful to think of them as "ours". To do so lessens our openness to them and an openness to such things is most urgently needed now and in the days ahead.

Walking out

Over the last couple of years I have been looking at reclamations in places like the Pearl River Delta and Tokyo Bay. On Shijō-mae, one of the more recent rectangular islands that comprise the 250 square kilometres of reclamation in Tokyo Bay, the ground is also mostly bare or has just a thin cover of grass. This island is one the most recent of a series of reclamations extending out from the former shoreline. On a stiflingly hot day in August 2016, walking out from the old city across three of these islands and across the bridges connecting them, I move from the 1910s to the 1920s and then to the 1960s, the time Shijō-mae was formed. It is like walking up through the stratigraphy of the twentieth century in a kind of reverse archaeology. Reaching Shijō-mae, where the tabula rasa effect is most evident and where the heat is beginning to muddle my mind, I imagine for a moment that the new terrain before me had been exposed by a retreating sea rather than by an advancing land (in other words, that the sea has gone out rather than the land).

Walking back

But the sea is advancing, not retreating, and implicit here is another walk, the walk back inland, the walk of regression or retreat. We know this walk – we've done it before.

When the sea around Australia was 125 meters lower than today, the coast off Sydney was between six and twenty kilometers east of where it is now. Aboriginal people are assumed to have occupied the undulating plain of the continental shelf lying exposed off Sydney at this time. As the glaciers and ice sheets elsewhere in the world began to melt, the sea moved back in over the land and those people retreated inland in front of the advancing sea, losing something like three meters of territory a year and presumably adjusting their clan territories as they went, as well as incrementally modifying their spiritual, storied, and economic understanding of the land. They would have witnessed how, at high tide, the sea edged further up the sandstone cliffs than it had before; how it crept up and over the edge

Denis Byrne

of the rock platforms on the seashore, filling nooks and cran-nies and running forward to create tidal pools where none had been before. They were weathering the effects of a Quaternary cycle whose Anthropocene version *we* are now asked to weather. To walk back, in other words, to a smaller space. This could be humiliating and liberating.

Either way, it is hard not to see that the rhythms that infect this paper – terrestrial expansion and contraction, ebb and flow, breathing in and breathing out, are here too.

Notes

1   For the most detailed account of European-Aboriginal contact in the early years of colonial settlement see Karskens (2009).

Works Cited

Barad, Karen. (2012). "Nature's Queer Performativity," Kvinder, Køn & Forshning 1-2, 25-53.

Connor, Steven. (n.d.). "Topologies: Michel Serres and the Shapes of Thought," http://www.stevenconnor.com/topologies/.

Deleuze, Gilles. (1993). *The Fold: Leibniz and the Baroque*. Trans. by Tom Conley. London: Continuum.

Ensor, Sarah. (2017). "Queer Fallout: Samuel R. Delany and the Ecology of Cruising." *Environmental Humanities* 9(1), 149-166.

Gandy, Mathew. (2012). "Queer Ecology: Nature, Sexuality, and Heterotopic Alliances." *Environment and Planning D* 30, 727–47.

Howe, Cymene. (2016). "Timely." In "Lexicon for an Anthropocene Yet Unseen," edited by Cymene Howe and Anand Pandian, Theorizing the Contemporary series, *Cultural Anthropology* website, January 21, retrieved from http://www.culanth.org/fieldsights/800-timely.

Karskens, Grace. (2009). *The Colony: A History of Early Sydney*. Sydney: Allen and Unwin.

Merleau-Ponty, Maurice. (1968). *The Visible and the Invisible*. Trans. by Alfonso Lingis. Evanston, IL: Northwestern University Press.

Serres, Michel. (1997). *Genesis*. Trans. by Genevieve James and James Nielson. Ann Arbor: University of Michigan Press.

Yusoff, Kathryn. (2016) ."Anthropogenesis: Origins and Endings in the Anthropocene." *Theory, Culture and Society* 33(2), 3-28.

Denis Byrne

14 A Manifesto for Creature Languages

Kate Wright

Because a lightning strike does not come down from the clouds in a continuous motion, but is instead emergent, and intra-active – formed in communication with the earth, Vicki Kirby describes it as a kind of 'stuttering chatter between ground and sky'.[1] As if gold scribbles through the crow black night – sharp and erratic, stop and start - like the tongue of one wracked with anxiety, to stall at the cliff-face of words, in the space between sound and silence.

And if the world is, as Kirby argues, a cacophonous conversation, perhaps the black ants that swirl around my feet like dots of ink nipping at my toes can be heard to sing "rain, rain, rain." Because I learned when I was a little kid that ants and water rhyme, because lines of ants across the pinewood of our kitchen bench were, almost always, followed by a chorus of rain and thunder. And much later in my life, Dharawal Elder, Aunty Frances Bodkin advised me that ants respond to weather conditions months in advance: 'Their nests go down to the groundwater' she said 'and groundwater is connected to air pressure, it rises and falls as the air pressure changes'.[2]

So it is that the moving architecture of an ant mount in response to weather– a multiplicity made of the microscopic bodies of the living and the dead coalescing with mineral rock and mobilised by an insect colony – can tell you which direction the rain is coming from. 'The world communicates itself as it creates itself'[3] and this language of life is what environmental philosopher Deborah Bird Rose refers to as 'creature languages'.

> The sight and smell of flowers, the pain of the march fly bite and the sensation of blood running down the leg, the sight of swifts in the sky or flower petals drifting in the river, fireflies winking and the interminable racket of cicadas: these are multifaceted creature languages,

and smart creatures take notice. Humans enhance their intelligence not by stepping out of the system and trying to control it, but by enmeshing themselves ever more knowledgeably into the creature-languages of Country.[4]

It is said that we have entered the 'Age of Man', where the collective agency of the human species has become geological - what Michel Serres has called 'the dense tectonic plates of humanity.'[5] With such emphasis on the newfound mineralogical coordinates of the human "event" it can sometimes go unremarked upon that the burning of fossil fuels is a mobilisation of creaturely powers – that the uncanny return of the dead bodies of our Carboniferous multispecies kin to feed our fossil economy is part of a collective material agency, as the human, ant-like, burrows into and releases the subterranean forces of the Earth. Hacking into the narcissistic edifice of the Anthropocene, as if chiselling into the granite to which a memory of our species is to be forever consigned, is a reminder that humans are always becoming-with nonhuman kin.

As a conceptual frame and an embodied political tactic, 'weathering' is a mode of attunement that attends to this relational becoming. In this immanent, affective, viscous approach to the living world, the more-than-human kin that surround us are part of a semiotic ecology – their own affective and responsive bodies reverberating with difference as they communicate shifts in time and place. Nonhuman bodies are both signals and agents because everything in the world 'is a kind of immanent process of mediation or communication,'[6] and an active participant in the world's becoming.

Yolngu Elder LakLak Burrarwanga describes multispecies weathering in a communicative more-than-human matrix through the coming of a storm:

> This lightning and thunder is sending out messages to other countries and other homelands telling everyone – Yolngu, animals, plants, everyone – that arra'mirri mayaltha [a particular season] is coming. Are you listening? Are you looking, smelling, feeling, tasting it? Quick Baru

Kate Wright

[crocodile] there's a message here for you, don't miss it. It's very hot and humid during the day now and we're starting to sweat during the night. The night sweating is a message, telling us fruit, like larani [apple] is getting ripe.[7]

It is a condition of existence that we cannot attend to all difference in our environments. As Uexküll observed through his concept of Umwelt – our sensory bubbles are always tuning out part of the rich ecologies we inhabit.[8] Attending to more-than-human semiotic ecologies – creature languages – is a way of picking up on important environmental change that we would never be able to perceive with our own, all too human, sensory apparatus.

While the bodies of our more-than-human kin are a crucial part of our epistemology, I think it is important that these bodies are not approached with an extractivist mindset, to be dissected and mined for information. Scholars involved in Indigenous language revitalisation talk about the dangers of extracting Indigenous languages from community and place, and inadvertently (or intentionally) inserting colonial or capitalist concepts.[9] Creature languages are minoritarian and counter-colonial. They are part of the ongoing differentiation of life. If, as Hugo Reinert observes, extractive resource capitalism is a sort of 'ontological machine—an engine that continuously remakes the world... in ways that facilitate surplus value extraction'[10] – creature languages help us to work against this destructive worlding, and ask us to think otherwise. In this sense, creature languages can be understood as part of an intersectional more-than-human counter-colonial struggle. This decolonisation of creaturely linguistics must attend to creature languages not as a *lingua nullius* – but as a semiotic field that is an integral part of First Nation cultures and knowledge systems, requiring genuine collaborative engagement with Indigenous thinkers.

Callum Clayton-Dixon, an Ambēyaŋ scholar and co-founder of the Anaiwan language revival program, argues that:

For Aboriginal people, language is not merely a tool for communicating and relating with other humans.

Language is also core to maintaining healthy relationships with country. The devastation inflicted upon Aboriginal languages by colonial violence, parallel to and interconnected with the colonisation of Aboriginal lands, lives and liberties, has caused extreme disruption to the fundamental relationships between people and country. It is therefore necessary, in principle and in practice, to ensure language revitalisation efforts aim to repatriate language to country. Like Indigenous peoples have been displaced from country, forced onto reserves and missions, Aboriginal languages have likewise been displaced from country, forced onto the pages of anthropologists' and linguists' notebooks, gathering dust in university and library archives.

Language revitalisation has a crucial role to play in contemporary assertions of Indigeneity, in what Cherokee academic Jeff Corntassel describes as the reclamation and regeneration of our 'relational place-based existence.'[12]

The Anaiwan Language Revival Program, an Aboriginal language revitalisation initiative in the so-called New England Tableland region of New South Wales, has begun the task of repatriating language to land by undertaking cultural site trips, reclaiming place names, and reconnecting lexical items with the elements of country to which they belong (e.g. plant and animal species). Language revitalisation ultimately offers a means of reclaiming and reviving the ancient reciprocal relationships we as Aboriginal people held within the natural world since the first sunrise.

Akarre Elder Margaret Kemarre Turner stated that "Language is a gift from that Land for the people who join into that Land... We come from the Land, and the language comes from the Land... language is born out of the living flesh of that Land" (Turner, 194). In other words, human language is not a property that separates

Kate Wright

humans from the nonhuman world, but an extension of the eloquence of life – and a gift.

Notes

1   Vicky Kirby, *Quantum Anthropologies: Life at Large* (Durham: Duke University Press, 2011) 10.

2   Frances Bodkin, cited in Kate Wright, *Transdisciplinary Journeys in the Anthropocene: More-than-Human Encounters* (Oxon and New York: Routledge, 2017) 162.

3   Andrew Murphie, "The World as Medium: Whitehead's Media Philosophy," *Immediation I,* eds. Erin Manning, Anne Munster and Bodil Marie Stavning Thomsen (London: Open Humanities Press, 2019) 16-46.

4   Deborah Bird Rose, 'Val Plumwood's Philosophical Animism: Attentive Interactions in the Sentient World,' *Environmental Humanities* 3 (2013): 104.

5   Michel Serres, *The Natural Contract,* trans. Elizabeth MacArthur and William Paulson (Ann Arbor: University of Michigan Press, 1995) 16.

6   Murphie, "The World as Medium."

7   Sarah Wright et al. "Telling Stories In, Through and With Country: Engaging with Indigenous and More-than-Human Methodologies at Bawaka NE Australia," *Journal of Cultural Geography* 29(1) (2012): 39-60.

8   Nineteenth-century biologist Jakob von Uexküll used the term Umwelt to describe the way organism and environment form a whole system. Each organism has its own Umwelt, which is its meaningful environment. See "A Stroll Through the Worlds of Animals and Men: A Picture Book of Invisible Worlds," *Instinctive Behavior: The Development of a Modern Concept,* ed. and trans. Claire H. Schiller (New York: International Universities Press, 1957) 5–80.

9   Simon Fraser University, *Decolonizing Language Revitalization.* Retrieved from summit.sfu.ca/item/14186 (2014).

10 Hugo Reinert, "About a Stone: Some Notes on Geologic Conviviality," *Environmental Humanities* 8(1) (2016): 96.

11 Margaret Kemarre Turner and Barry McDonald Perrurle *Iwenhe Tyerrtye*: What it Means to be an Aboriginal person, trans. Veronica Perrurle Dobson (Alice Springs: IAD Press, 2010).

12   Jeff Corntassel, "Re-envisioning Resurgence: Indigenous Pathways to Decolonization and Sustainable Self-Determination," *Decolonization: Indigeneity, Education and Society* 1(1) (2012): 88.

Works Cited

Clayton-Dixon, Callum. Personal Communication, Armidale, 9 December, 2017.

Corntassel, Jeff. (2012). "Re-envisioning Resurgence: Indigenous Pathways to Decolonization and Sustainable Self-Determination." *Decolonization: Indigeneity, Education and Society* 1(1), 86-101.

Kirby, Vicki. (2011). *Quantum Anthropologies: Life at Large*. Durham: Duke University Press.

Murphie, Andrew. (2019). "The World as Medium: Whitehead's Media Philosophy." In *Immediation I,* eds. Erin Manning, Anne Munster and Bodil Marie Stavning Thomsen (London: Open Humanities Press. 16-46.

Reinert, Hugo. (2016). "About a Stone: Some Notes on Geologic Conviviality." *Environmental Humanities* 8(1), 95-117.

Rose, Deborah Bird. (2013). "Val Plumwood's Philosophical Animism: Attentive Interactions in the Sentient World," *Environmental Humanities* 3, 94-109.

Serres, Michel. (1995). *The Natural Contract.*, trans: Elizabeth MacArthur and William Paulson. Ann Arbor: University of Michigan Press.

Simon Fraser University. (2014). *Decolonizing Language Revitalization*. Retrieved from summit.sfu.ca/item/14186.

Turner, Margaret Kemarre. (2010). *Iwenhe Tyerrtye: What it Means to be an Aboriginal Person*. Trans. Barry McDonald Perrurl & Veronica Perrurle Dobson. Alice Springs: IAD Press.

von Uexküll, Jacob. (1957). "A Stroll Through the Worlds of Animals and Men: A Picture Book of Invisible Worlds." In *Instinctive Behavior: The Development of a Modern Concept*, ed. and trans. Claire H. Schiller. New York: International Universities Press. 5–80.

Wright, Kate. (2017). *Transdisciplinary Journeys in the Anthropocene: More-than-human Encounters*. Oxon and New York: Routledge.

Wright, Sarah., Kate Lloyd, Sandie Suchet-Pearson, Laklak Burrarwanga and Matalena Tofa. (2012). "Telling Stories In, Through and With Country: Engaging with Indigenous and More-than-Human Methodologies at Bawaka NE Australia." *Journal of Cultural Geography* 2(1), 39-60.

15 Lifejackets: Future Fossils of the Anthropocene?

Cameron Muir

For a little over six months I corresponded with Tasos Markou, a freelance photographer from Greece who is documenting the refugee crisis in the Mediterranean.

Tasos's work there began in the summer of 2015, when he went to the island of Lesvos, and drove north to the tiny fishing village of Skala Sikamineas. From tavernas clustered by the shore here you can see Turkey across the Aegean Sea. On the beach, Tasos saw shoes, backpacks, T-shirts, plastic water bottles and lifejackets.

Tasos told me, "I realised this was not just rubbish. Each life jacket meant a human life, a story of a crossing."

You can buy a factory-direct child's life jacket online for US $4.14 apiece. Shipping is free to most destinations. Lifejackets say something about how it feels to live in these times. The orange colour is a signal for help; it communicates the courage and desperation of people on the move, hopes dashed at the borders while the rest of us watch on feeling powerless.

At the end of summer Tasos returned to Lesvos. The little island was now receiving 200,000 people per month.

Locals made a space in the cemetery for refugees.

Fishermen in Skala Sikamineas spent the nights in their boats, guiding refugees to the shore, diving into the water and rescuing people. Women gave sandwiches and fruit. They hugged and kissed those who made the crossing.

In an interview with the UK-based NGO Help Refugees, fisherman Stratos Valiamos said, 'These people have started a journey to a better life. 'I will not let the sea stop them.'[1]

Tasos quit freelancing for the agencies and newspapers and became a volunteer.

I thought about the response these refugees and migrants would have received in Australia.

Refugees have been represented as dangerous for wealthy nations and, in the words Alex Randall of the UK Climate Change and Migration Coalition, as 'agents of chaos in the Middle East.' Some commentators have pointed to links between climate change and the conflict in Syria, warning the future will bring more terrorism and hordes of climate change refugees overwhelming countries and causing the collapse of states.[2]

Randall pointed out that drought in Syria didn't make people turn on each other – it united them. Different groups began mingling in urban centres in a way that Assad's regime had tried to prevent. This led to protests and cooperation, which Assad's authoritarian government responded to with violence.

It the dynamics of the Anthropocene, more than climate change, that you can see in the context for Syria. People making a few dollars an hour produce cheap PVC and Polyester safety vests and inflatable boats that are shipped around the world and resold to desperate refugees fleeing conflict, poverty and ecological disorder for the security of Europe, the United States, and Australia. The refugees come from places that the wealthy countries are bombing in wars that are in part a legacy of Europe's late-imperialist carve-up of territory, forced migrations, exploitation of fossil fuels, Cold War geopolitics, a postcolonial distortion of Islam backed by Saudi oil money, failed mega-irrigation projects, depletion of groundwater, Assad's neoliberal economic restructure, and the rise of the privatised corporate war economy under the auspices of the War on Terror.

Ethemcan Turhan and Marco Armiero argue we are operating with 'lifeboat' ethics.[3] In the affluent countries we pretend it's possible to escape the social and environmental disruption of the Anthropocene in our lifeboats while the displaced clamour to get on board in their cheap lifejackets.

Lifejackets piled up at the borders might become future fossils, the material remains of our Anthropocene politics.

On the other hand, instead of creating fortresses and retreating to xenophobic nationalism, what if we saw our grievances as shaped by the same larger forces? These play out differently in local places and the burden is unequal, but what if we recognised the real threat are the few who benefit the greatest from Anthropocene politics; that most of us are on the same side?

Could we seek solidarity with refugees and migrants? Rather treating refugees as security threats, requiring militarised solutions, could we see migration as an adaptation to the challenges of the Anthropocene?

Permissions

An extended version of this text appears in *Griffith Review Edition* 57: Perils of Populism, 'The Remixing of Peoples: Migration as Adaptation' (July 2017).

Notes

1   Help Refugees, "Lighthouse - Refugee Relief on Lesvos, Talks to Stratos Valiamos." *Facebook,* 4 Feb. 2016. https://www. facebook.com/HelpRefugeesUK/posts/lighthouse-refugee-relief-on-lesvos-talks-to-stratos-valiamos-one-of-the-fisherm/184317828595565/. Accessed 1 Aug. 2019.

2   See, for example, *The Age of Consequences*, a 2016 documentary promoted as "*The Hurt Locker* meets An *Inconvenient Truth.*"*The Age of Consequences*. Directed by Jared P. Scott, PF Pictures, 27 Jan. (2017).

3   Turhan, Ethemcan, and Marco Armiero. "Cutting the Fence, Sabotaging the Border: Migration as a Revolutionary Practice." *Capitalism Nature Socialism* 28(2) (2017): 4.

Works Cited

The Age of Consequences. Directed by Jared P. Scott, PF Pictures, 27 Jan. 2017.

Help Refugees, "Lighthouse - Refugee Relief on Lesvos, Talks to Stratos Valiamos." *Facebook,* 4 Feb. 2016, retrieved from https://www.facebook.com/HelpRefugeesUK/posts/lighthouse-refugee-relief-on-lesvos-talks-to-stratos-valiamos-one-of-the-fisherm/184317828595565/. Accessed 1 Aug. 2019.

Turhan, Ethemcan, and Marco Armiero. (2017). "Cutting the Fence, Sabotaging the Border: Migration as a Revolutionary Practice." *Capitalism Nature Socialism* 28(2), 1-9.

Cameron Muir

16 take a parcel of ocean

Susan Reid

I sometimes follow the night breeze from Canberra to the coast, travelling the familiar route along the Kings Highway and cutting through the beautiful carbon-rich Monga and Budawang National Parks. Fragrances of sassafras, tree ferns, red gums and leaf litter give way to a soft scented ocean breeze as the range drops down to the coast. Street lights dangle like anglerfish lures between grabs of pale-brick sea-side investments, 24-hour servos and slow-to-close taverns.

Riding the breeze over a ruffled ocean skin, well beyond the bay and remnant estuaries, I arrive at one of the immense 200 kilometre-wide eddies stirring offshore. As it spins, the eddy pushes warm surface water from its core, making way for cooler, upwelled water from the seafloor. Particles and creatures imperceptibly transition as they glide over and through one another: chemical and minerals, sand granules and organic nutrients, fish eggs, leaf litter, bits of plastic, weed, and larvae, collected from the continental shelf, entrained to the surface and stirred in a great rotating parcel of water.

Whether I float above, or sink vertically into this slow-turning, massive column of water, facing into it there is no sense of its beginning. Neither does following the flow find an end or past. Suspended in the eddy, against its powerful, sinewy jets, I can taste briny solution coursing through me, front to back. Tiny bits of me fall away into the flow. Incremental changes in temperature have already begun, only now I notice them. As I cool, the water nearer my body warms. My entire skin covering is now porous to the ocean. Water fills my mouth, pushes through old gills, squeezes oxygen into capillaries; I am streaming with ocean. Moving across the eddy, I sense changes in temperature and current strength. There is no border as such, no set moment when I am in the eddy and then out of it.

Transitioning ocean currents continue to change how they move around the planet; and now strengthening carbon flows from our emissions bring change of a different register. In some places slower and weaker in response to thermohaline dilution or stronger, as with the East Australian Current, sending warmer water southward.

Plumes of greenhouse gases rise unseen above the landscape, every day, everywhere. Carbon bodies bonded to our terrestrian lives crowd the atmosphere and swamp its dispersive capacity. Beneath the thickening carbon blanket, the stewing ocean plumps on streams of fallen carbon bodies drawn in through its skin, travelling on the back of currents and sinking with spent phytoplankton to the sediment below.

Abstractions allow us to think and imagine (Stengers 2011) and in the opening image, I want to think with and imagine my way into feeling the transitional nature of the ocean's watery dynamics; to feel my body's transitional, "transcorporeal" nature (Alaimo 2010, 2). Hanging on to remnant ideas of bodily integrity avoid necessary reckoning with the shady carbon by-products of my existence.

How I am transitioning now signals future transitions. Yet I do not know how to reckon fully with the carbon by-products of being me; neither can I recognise, or know how to transition with, my growing carbon others. How long does one continue to stay with the trouble (Haraway 2016).

Switching on the ignition, I follow the same route over Country ribboned with hydrocarbon. Over the entire journey, fuel sloshes in the tank, mingles with oxygen, combusts, and is steadily exhaled. Invisibly exhaust particles settle road-side grasses and low-hanging branches. Lighter particles drift skyward with other gases already thickening the atmosphere. Winding down the window invites a rush of exhaust ahead of sassafras, red gum and leaf litter fragrances. Hydrocarbon traces from my emissions and hard plastic dashboard hold fast inside, others flush out on breeze or breathe.

Susan Reid

By the time I pass over the Great Dividing Range to the coast, my car has dumped around 30kilograms of carbon dioxide alone into the atmosphere – about half my body weight. A return trip produces an entire body weight in carbon dioxide. In going about the Earth for 30 odd years, co-extensive with various cars, I have created close to 750 such carbon bodies… enough to form another gassy political party.

My abstracted sense of bodily integrity can only operate in the absence of a co-generation with the world, or of "worlding"(Haraway, 2016 10) or "weathering" (Neimanis and Walker, 2014, 558). So too, in Anthropocenic discourses bodily integrity moves under the thrall of climate change, affected by it, adapting to it, mitigating against it. But as I go about my Terrestrian ways, and unhinge my relation with this integrity, there emerges other, not so strange, 'intra-active' carbon bodies with which I transition in and make relations with.

Follow the smoky night breeze to the coast, along the sun-softened tar of the Kings Highway, and cutting through new growth patches in the Monga and Budawang National Parks. Fragrances of sassafras, red gums and of a night damp charry give way to a briny wind, as the range drops down to the coast. Its Eastern slopes now checkered with concrete Cat 6 bunkers and scraggly banana tree patches.

Angled solar lights festoon the sea-walled bay and strong gusts chop at the ocean's skin; there's no sign of the estuaries. Offshore, my broad carbon body hazes above one of many churning eddies. Warm microbial water pushes away beneath us, as a slow tongue of cooler water upwells from the seafloor.

Particles and creatures imperceptibly transition as they glide over and through one another: chemicals and minerals, new fish arrivals, faecal matter and other organic surprises; jellyfish eggs knocked from the retaining walls, algal clumps and chunks of archival plastic, plastic and more plastic; all swept from the lengthening shelf, entrained to the surface, and stirred in a thickening parcel of water.

At the eddy's edge, another of my fallen carbon bodies struggles to fully disassemble into this massive column of swirling carbon soup. She and I stumble and collapse into one another, bit by tiny bit. We're mixing into the warm flow; current bodies streaming my carbon.

Works Cited

Alaimo, S. (2010). *Bodily Natures: Science, Environment and the Material Self*. Indiana, U.S.A.: Indiana University Press.

Haraway, D. J. (2016). *Staying with the Trouble: Making Kin in the Chthulucene*. Durham & London: Duke University Press.

Neimanis, A., and Hamilton, J. (2017). "The weather is now political." Retrieved June 12, 2018, from http://theconversation.com/the-weather-is-now-political-77791

Neimanis, A., & Loen Walker, R. (2014). "Weathering: Climate Change and the 'Thick Time' of Transcorporeality." *Hypatia*, 29(3), 558–575.

Stengers, I. (2011). *Thinking with Whitehead: A Free and Wild Creation of Concepts*. United States: Harvard University Press.

Susan Reid

17   A Week on the Cooks River

Clare Britton

Rejected in favour of the Parramatta River and Sydney Harbour, the Cooks River is not the body of water that comes to mind when thinking about Sydney.[1] Historian Paul Carter points out in *The Road to Botany Bay: An Exploration of Landscape and History* that Botany Bay (and by extension the Cooks River) is one of Australia's first "Other" places: "Botany Bay, the name no sooner makes history than it is eclipsed, left astern. It ends as it began, a rhetorical place." The Cooks is technically a tidal estuary not a river and flows twenty-three kilometres from Yagoona to Botany Bay. Rain gathers at the lowest points of a valley into a ribbon of water that meets with the brackish daily tides. Over its course, the water moves by Sydney's largest cemetery, suburban houses, Indigenous middens and cave shelters, an ice-skating rink and industrial areas. The river is named after Captain James Cook and its mouth was engineered a kilometre off-course, in the late 1940s, to make way for Sydney's Kingsford Smith International Airport.

In my experience, when people get excited talking about the Cooks River it includes visceral descriptions of how it smells at low tide or of the remarkable things they have seen floating in the water. I have seen cars, bikes, a Vespa, shopping trolleys and a teddy bear larger than a person— matted, sodden and face down in the mangroves. Anecdotes I have heard include sightings of a lounge suite and dead animals—a horse's head, a pig and dogs. To borrow from Bachelard's *Poetics of Space* by thinking about the Cooks River through the metaphor of a home, the Cooks River is more like looking down the back of Sydney's couch as opposed to greeting Sydney at its front door. As the Cooks River is somewhat unconsidered, it holds uncomfortable truths. Standing on the bank of the Cooks, its trajectory is hard to perceive as a whole. Despite the many colonial, urban and suburban compromises the Cooks River has absorbed, it is strangely beautiful. Its beauty is complicated and delicate. If you soften your eyes and look out along the water as the sun is setting, you might see a mullet throw itself out of the golden pinky water and imagine what it would feel like to swim down to Tempe railway station instead of walking there. If you look closely at the water you might notice a slick, a dense tangle of plastic, a Keep Cup floating downstream or you might make out the shape of an O-Bike on the riverbed; this doesn't account for the pollution you can't see.

I walked, observed and rowed the Cooks over, 4 years. On a bush walking track that follows Wolli Creek to the Cooks River I collected several small objects: a flake of rust from the barbie at Wanstead reserve, a casuarina seed cone, a Sydney cockle shell, a piece of plastic from the lid of a water bottle. These small objects, cast in silver, reflect a desire to draw attention to the river and to value things around us that are easy to overlook. I made a collection of casts and gave them away to people who walked with me. This sculpture has atomised. Every now and then I get an update about where a piece has travelled. There are a couple of Sydney cockle shells in the UK. One flake of rust has stayed in a Yurt in France. There are gum nuts in Slovenia and one on the North Coast of New South Wales that is put outside every full moon. There is a piece of BBQ debris in a pocket in Wollongong; a mud welch that fell off a trolley while moving office and is still missing. I like to think about where they all are. The following photo essay starts with an image of the small silver sculptures and then follows the Cooks River underwater from Strathfield Golf Course to Botany Bay (Figures 1- 10).

The Cooks River with Clare and Sally[3]

Interview by Alexandra Crosby

I don't often get boating invitations. This week, when Clare Britton asked me to climb aboard the newly renovated 'Sally' at the Tempe Pier (see Figure 11), I didn't hesitate. As part of her research project A Week on the Cooks River, Clare is spending time observing, describing, rowing the Cooks.

AC: So can you tell me what you brought?

CB: I've got two cameras. One is for shooting underwater – I can attach it to the side of the boat; and my digital SLR, which I have with me- both take stills and video. I borrowed a zoom audio recorder. I have a raincoat, 500ml of SPF 50+ (sensitive) sun cream, a water bottle, muesli bars, a hat and then, books, drawing materials and a logbook.

AC: And how about the boat?

CB: *Sally* is a little fibreglass dinghy. Painted blue-green on the inside and white outside with a wood seat and trim. I did some renovations in preparation for the week on the river because the boat is second hand and the wood frame was rotted. I took the existing trim as a pattern and went through with the radial arm saw and cut a series of small grooves into long lengths of wood so I could bend it around the boat. Before the side would flex quite a lot, now its a lot more solid. The boat was in the workshop (at Sydney College of the Arts) for about a week while I worked on it. I had to go to the marine supplies shop to get stainless steel bolts, screws and varnish because the river is salty water and the old ones were really rusty.

• • •

I take over the oars so Clare can film some jellyfish. The movement is unfamiliar. I am going backwards, which is not a problem except when there are obstacles. For a moment the bridge blocks the light, and I try to control the drift, to weave between the pylons- it's not dangerous, Clare reminds me, just unsettling. We are going very slowly and gently (see Figure 12).

Figure 1. "A Week on the Cook's River" Silver castings of objects collected on the Cooks River (dimensions variable 20-40mm).

Clare Britton

Figure 2. Underwater in Strathfield Golf Club.

Figure 3. Underwater in Strathfield Golf Club.

Figure 4. Mangroves on the river bed in Dulwhich Hill.

Figure 5. Submerged plastic in Marrickville.

Clare Britton

Figure 6. Ride share bike in the river in Earlwood.

Figure 7. Mangrove seed.

Clare Britton

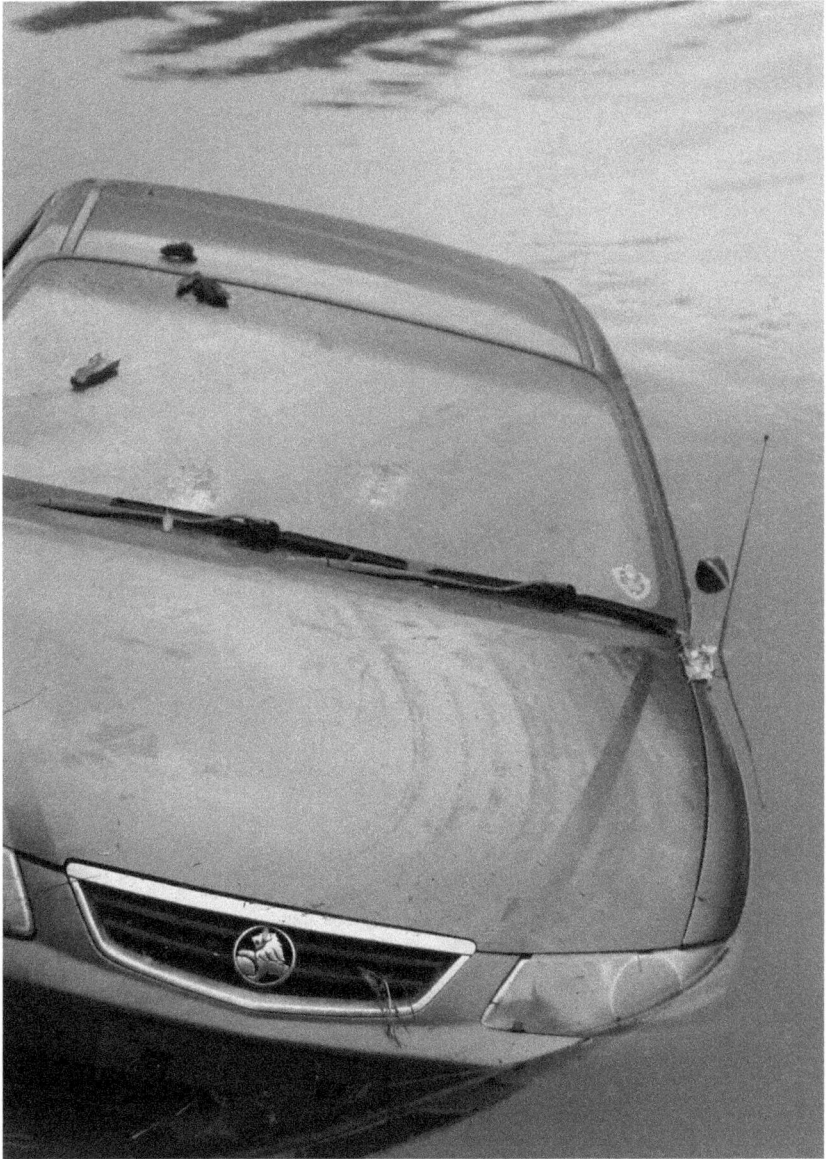

Figure 8. Holden sedan at Gough Whitlam Park.

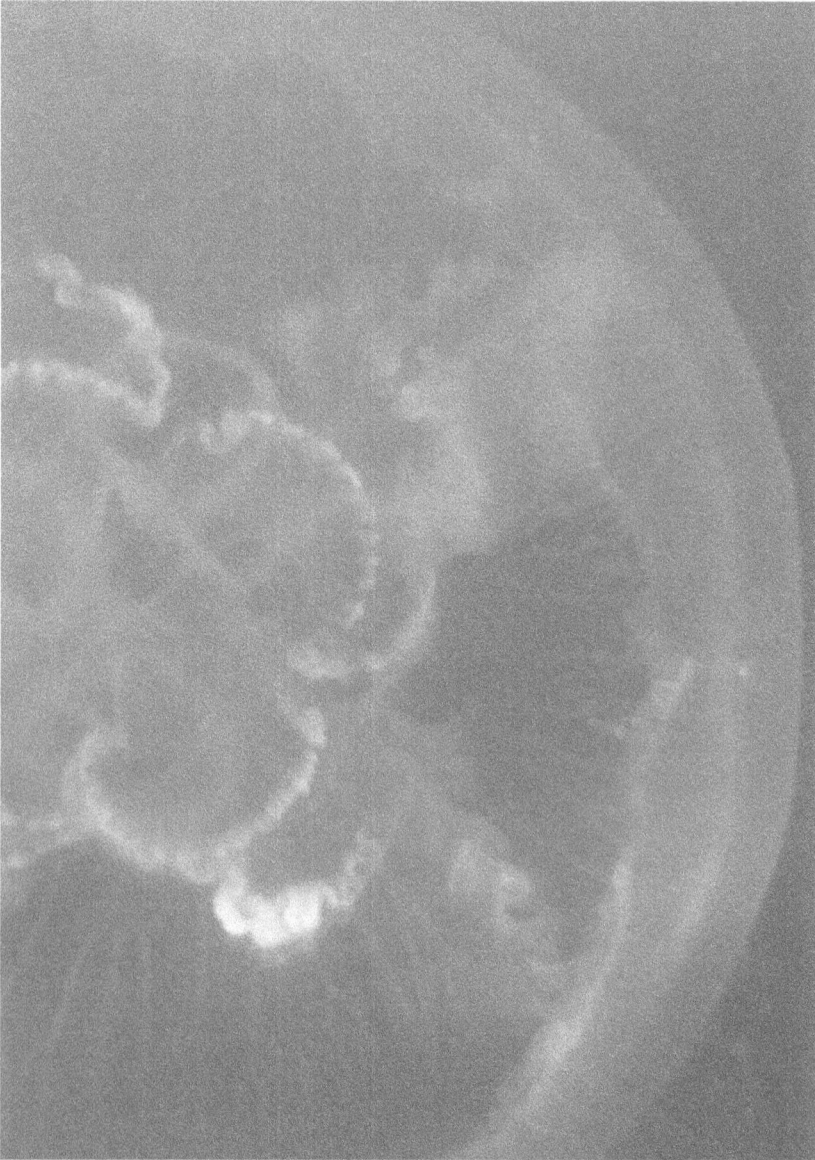

Figure 9. Jelly fish at Tempe.

Clare Britton

Figure 10. Deep water near Botany Bay.

CB: It's high tide, so it doesn't matter where we go under the bridge, but if its low tide, you have to go in the middle. I haven't been scared about it, but you can run aground when the water is low. I've hit oysters. I rowed up to Canterbury ice rink against the tide, and it took me so long. Some sections are very gentle, though, like little swirls.

AC: Better to go with the tide then?

CB: Yes – much easier. Yesterday I decided to drift, I literally pulled the oars up near Gough Whitlam Park, and I thought 'let's just see what happens', and (the water) carried me down under the bridge near Tempe station, it spun the boat slowly around a few times and then took me along Wolli Creek. Now the tide is going out, so we are doing the opposite of what the water wants us to do.

AC: Where are we now?

CB: This little clump of mangrove trees is Fatima Island. This side is the suburb Wolli Creek and that side is Kendrick Park, Tempe. Kendrick Park is the site of one of the most significant middens

Figure 11. Boat at Tempe Boat Ramp. Photo by Matt Prest.

Clare Britton

Figure 12. Shopping trolley in the river at Tempe.

in this area. When it was colonised, they built a lime-burning kiln, near where Tempe station is now and burned a lot of that midden to get lime for the early colonial buildings. Ironically, this whole part over here, where all the new buildings are going up near Wolli Creek station, is called Discovery Point.

AC: How have you been handling the days in the week?

CB: The vague structure is that I want to go all the way from Yagoona to Botany Bay, to follow the river out the sea. Monday I walked from Yagoona to Earlwood. Tuesday I went to Tempe and rowed up to Canterbury ice rink then rowed back down. Wednesday I went up Muddy Creek, which is near the Market Gardens at Kyeemagh. Yesterday I went up Wolli Creek. Today I'm just noodling around in this area. Tomorrow is the Alexandra Canal, and on Sunday I'm going all the way to Botany Bay. Besides today, I have been alone all the time. Today is about talking to people and taking a few friends out for a little explore.

AC: And you've been describing as you go?

CB: Yes, using audio recordings. I really want to do a description of the river, from Yagoona to Botany Bay. I've been recording, sitting in my boat or in places along the river and describing it. It's a tool for me, so I remember it all when I am working in my studio and on my computer again. I've tried some solar plate etching too, I've just been sort of keeping track of what's been going on. The two books I've had with me are: 'Gadigal Country' edited by Anita Heiss. And this ancient tome, Thoreau's book 'A Week on the Concord and Merrimac Rivers'.

• • •

There is one essay of Thoreau's called 'Walking' and this part I have been thinking about where he says...If you are ready to leave father and mother, and brother and sister, and wife and child and friends, and never see them again if you have paid your debts, and made your will, and settled all your affairs, and are a free man then, you are ready for a walk.

I've been turning it over – and thinking about it as an artist, but also a suburban mum, how does it translate? I'm very attracted to the idea, the sense of adventure. Can I do a version of that here? (and also attend the local High School's new parent/student information session?)

• • •

Clare gracefully takes over so I can take a few pics of the Wolli Creek high rise. Her movements seem effortless. What was I doing wrong?

CB: Well, you can push with your feet as well and use the weight of the top part of your body to pull back. And the rhythm- going a bit faster is easier. Your arms kind of stay stiff. I have developed some new muscles, and have blisters on my hands... You make your arms like a hard L, and then you move your whole body back... I don't really know what I'm doing I've just been doing what seems to work for me. When I was in Muddy Creek, the water was going in the opposite direction, and I was doing all I could to get back out. If I'd waited for the wind and the water to

Clare Britton

turn around it would have been so much easier, but I needed to go, and I just had to figure out how to get back in charge, and it's a pretty gentle river, so it's OK.... I've been enjoying it so much I don't want to go back to normal life!

AC: What is so different in normal life?

CB: Yesterday, I just put the oars up, and read two books and drifted around on the river. It's pretty rare I can spend a whole day like that in normal life. I feel like I have to get things done!

Doing this research, like Mapping Edges, is a way to be in the world, instead of racing around working through an absurd list of stuff. This week, for me, has been about getting a deeper sense of where I am. Everything in our lives, and the city, is against just being in the landscape – when I have stopped for long times along the river, I have felt a bit conspicuous – like people notice you're not really going somewhere and find it a bit disconcerting. I'll spend time stopping like that looking at the ocean or doing a bushwalk, but I don't really do it at home.

AC: What else has have you noticed?

CB: The tides and how different they make the river (it's really a tidal estuary, not a river as such). At low tide, the river is much shallower than I expected- only 20 or 30cms of water in some parts- it's quite thin. One thing that I used to think was that it was magic to see a fish jump out of the water. Being here day after day, I've realised it happens ten times a day like- it's very normal.

I've also noticed the mangroves. The seeds are floating about now- the river is full of mangrove seeds. There is a boat up Wolli Creek, and mangrove roots have grown all around it (see Figure 13) I didn't realise that mangrove roots, grow straight up. It's incredible how exactly like hairbrushes they are, the water moves through them and they just brush all the crap out of it.

We row past a split in the river.

AC: What happens if you go down there?

Figure 13. Mangroves and boat on Wolli Creek.

CB: I think it goes to the Sydenham reservoir, behind Supré. I'm curious about that little drain too, but I have to be a bit careful of those impulses, I don't really know how the reservoir works, and I can just see a newspaper headline 'Idiot artist dies in storm-water drain'.

• • •

Then I take the oars again, so Clare can use her phone. I hold my arms and back straight. I feel stronger. More in control. 'I think it's just about being a little bit more bossy with the rowing' Clare says. And I steer us gently to the Canoe Club where Clare picks up her next boating guests.

Notes

1   This writing acknowledges Traditional Owners and pays respect to past, present and future Elders. Emptying into Botany Bay, the site of Australia's colonisation, Sydney's Cooks River moves through the Country of the Wangal, Cadigal and Gameygal people.

2   Paul Irish, *Aboriginal History Along the Cooks River* (Sydney: Cooks River Alliance, 2017), 11.

Clare Britton

3   The Cooks River with Clare and Sally was originally published on "Mapping Edges." University of Technology, Sydney, http://www.mappingedges.org/conversations/cooks-river-clare-sally-conversations/. Accessed on 19th April 2020.

Works Cited

Bachelard, Gaston. (1994). *The Poetics of Space.* Boston: Beacon Press.

Carter, Paul. (1987). *The Road to Botany Bay. An Essay in Spatial History.* London: Faber and Faber.

Irish, Paul. (2017). *Aboriginal History Along the Cooks River.* Sydney: Cooks River Alliance.

Thoreau, Henry David. (1999). *Walking.* Boulder Colorado: Net Library.

Thoreau, Henry David. (1889). *A Week on the Concord and Merrimac Rivers.* London Walter Scott Ltd.

Tyrell, Ian. (2018). *River Dreams the People and Landscape of the Cooks River.* Sydney: New South Publishing.

Photographs by Clare Britton unless otherwise attributed.

18 Future of Fashion: A Manifesto

Lisa Heinze

Trend forecaster Li Edelkoort declared "fashion is dead" in her 2015 Anti-Fashion Manifesto. She suggested the industry has become too insular, students are only taught to be individualistic catwalk designers, the pace has accelerated too rapidly, textile design skills have been lost, sweatshops plague the industry, and fashion bloggers have taken over true fashion critique. While I agree with many of her gripes about the industry, I wholeheartedly disagree with her conclusion. I don't think fashion will ever be dead, and I don't think we should want it to be, either. It is far more productive to consider the creativity and innovation that are the hallmarks of fashion as invaluable skills for solving the many shortcomings of the industry, particularly the social and environmental devastation it causes.

These productive traits of fashion are also useful for weathering the end of the world as we know it as we forge into the Anthropocene – an ideal time to change the way things are done. Fashion solutions may be able to offer both physical and social comfort as we adjust to new norms. With that in mind, I will now present the beginnings of a Future of Fashion Manifesto.

Clear Connections

"Transparency" has become a sustainable fashion buzzword as fashion brands start to uncover their deep, global and complex supply chains. But a truly sustainable future of fashion means not only knowing who and where your suppliers are, but also forming connections with them. Two examples of radical transparency among Australian sustainable fashion labels include Carlie Ballard and Pure Pod.

Carlie Ballard uses a workshop in Lucknow, India to create her handwoven Ikat garments (see Figure 1). She personally visits the workshop annually and is constant contact with the workshop via email and Skype – as a sole proprietor and sustainable

Figure 1. Artisan fabric weavers in Lucknow, India, creating fabric for Carlie Ballard label. Photo by Christopher Ross for Carlie Ballard.

fashion start-up, finances do not support multiple trips per year. The workshop includes an onsite crèche, encourages entire garments to be sewn by one person, as opposed to traditional fashion factories that have workers sew the same seam over and over, and boasts female tailors, previously unheard of in the region. Importantly, the workspace and conditions were co-created with the workers themselves – the workshop was initially fitted with tables and desks, but the people explained that they are more comfortable sitting on the floor, and so the workshop adapted to suit their desires.

Kelli Donovan of Pure Pod (see Figure 2) has a similarly open relationship with her makers, though they are based in Australia. As she explains:

Figure 2. PurePod label on the runway at Undress Runways. Photo by Kelli Donovan of PurePod.

> With all of our makers, we end up having a very personal relationship as well. It's not just that we're sending it off to a factory, we end up caring about them, we have a very close relationship, [and I] always want to make sure they're being looked after. [For example, with my tailor], I give him chicken manure, and he gives us vegetables, and we give him eggs from our chickens.

Collaborative Kinship

Weathering an unstable future will be made possible by forming strong social bonds. In the fashion industry this can be seen through collaborative kinship – viewing other businesses not strictly as competitors but collaborators, and considering the emotional needs of the customer as well. I have found collaboration (see Figure 3) to be a hallmark of the sustainable fashion movement in my research with the Australian industry, especially amongst entrepreneurs.

Designer Kelli Donovan of Pure Pod is a pioneer in the industry. Her latest collection is not only Organic and Fairtrade

Lisa Heinze

Figure 3. Kowtow Collective on the runway at the Clean Cut Designer Showcase 2014. Photo by Lisa Heinze.

certified, but the print was created in collaboration with local artist Lauren Andersen, whose design aesthetic is underpinned by a love of Australian flora – working together strengthens the aesthetic possibilities as well as the social connections between Donovan and Andersen.

Donovan also forms connections with customers – strengthening social bonds on either end of the production/consumption process.

> I'll get women into the studio and some of them I'll have them in tears. [Because] they'll go to those fast fashion stores, they don't get service, [and] the clothes don't fit properly. And they get self-conscious and then they won't buy anything. Then they'll come to me and I'll either make them something or I'll give them a whole new wardrobe. Make them try on things they'd never try on, and they walk out and they're [happy and feel good about themselves]. If I can make a woman feel good about what they're wearing, they'll feel good in their health and wellbeing as well.

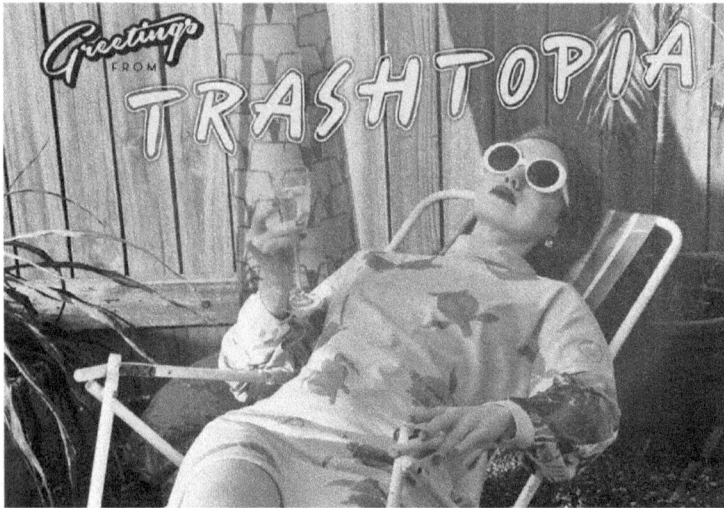

Figure 4. Trashtopia Collection Brisbane Resort 2014 /Dress made from recycled secondhand t-shirts. Hand block-printed. Buttons made from soy sauce fish. Photo by Carla van Lunn.

For Donovan this connection with customers is an integral part of her design practice, which brings joy to her and her customers. In fact, one of Donovan's clients came up to her during our interview in her favourite local café – she looked equal parts humbled and chuffed as she introduced us to each other and explained what Pure Pod items the woman was wearing. This is more than a job for financial gain.

(re)Creation

Rethinking waste is one of the most impactful means of weathering a future with overflowing landfills. Experimental label Maison Briz Vegas (see Figures 4-5) was influenced in part by Gay Hawkins' *Ethics of Waste* (2006) and actively works with waste to overcome the guilt associated with it and work towards an enchantment with waste. As Carla Binotto, one half of the duo explains, "A constant motivation for the two designers is transforming the humble and discarded into something rich and beautiful" (Binotto & Payne, 2017). The pieces are made of clothing from second-hand markets found on the outskirts of Paris. Embellished with hand-block

Figure 5. Trashtopia Collection Brisbane Resort 2014/Detail of dress hem made from plastic rubbish, shells, and glass beads. Photo by Carla van Lunn.

prints and plastic bag feathering, the label adheres to sustainable and slow fashion ideologies but also includes another motive, "an underlying desire to draw beauty and magic out of waste and excess" (Binotto & Payne, 2017).

Sheila Forever Intimates also re-thinks waste in her use of deadstock and offcut fabrics and minimal waste design. In traditional fashion manufacturing up to 20 per ent of the fabric is wasted on the cutting room floor (Rissanen & McQuillan, 2016) and traditional fashion production orders 20 per cent more fabric than is needed for a production run "just in case".

In the global market, outdoor apparel brand Patagonia is constantly on the cutting-edge of fashion innovation and technology, including re-thinking waste. It actively invests in innovation including recycling fabrics and plastics to create new garments, such as recycled nylon jackets, Nano-fluff jackets using recycled plastic for insulation, and down vests made with down they have recovered from comforters and pillows.

Challenge

The creativity of fashion can be used to challenge us all to think about the world in a different way. Many sustainable fashion labels include stories on swingtags or websites, and their Instagram feeds have a mixture of fashion beauty shots with information about the industry. Maison Briz Vegas offers an ideal example of challenging and provoking people through their Trashtopia collection. Slippers embellished with plastic from old milk jugs, feathers made of plastic bags, sequins and embellishments made of trash, all provoke new thinking not only about the way we view fashion, but the way we view waste – thought-provoking fashion leads to provoking thoughts about sustainability, life and our role on the planet.

Celebrate Creativity

In closing – fashion is part of life. To claim it is "dead" and should be forgotten neglects the magic it offers and its impact on how we view the world. So let's not toss it all away, or write it off as frivolous, wasteful or self-serving. Tapping into creativity is essential for weathering our future realities. Inspiration for responses to the Anthropocene can and must come from all aspects of social life, and fashion offers a prime opportunity to provoke new ways of thinking through its ability to attract, bewilder and inspire.

Works Cited

Binotto, C., & Payne, A. (2017). "The Poetics of Waste: Contemporary Fashion Practice in the Context of Wastefulness. *Fashion Practice* 9(1), 5-29, retrieved from doi:10.1080/17569370.2016.1226604

Edelkoort, L. (2015). "Anti-fashion manifesto." Retrieved from http://www.edelkoort.com/2015/09/anti_fashion-manifesto/

Hawkins, G. (2006). *The Ethics of Waste: How We Relate to Rubbish.* Oxford, England: Rowman & Littlefield.

Rissanen, T., & McQuillan, H. (2016). *Zero Waste Fashion Design.* London: Bloomsbury.

Lisa Heinze

19 On Hacking and Being Hacked

Annie Werner

I tend to agree with Sandra Steingraber when she suggests that cancer is as much a characteristic of the Anthropocene as climate change. We live in an era when we can no longer be surprised when our neighbour dies from bone cancer at the age of 13. When a friend of a friend gives birth to a baby already full of cancer. Or when a seemingly well 34 year old is diagnosed with off-the-charts aggressive breast cancer.

So given cancer's prominence in our age, its dominance in the cultural narratives that help us to understand and negotiate our selves, why am I telling this story?

Because telling a story about cancer as weathering not fighting, cancer treatment as queering, not battling, is resistance. Because "the available structures ... for storying illness can make and keep us ignorant about cancer" (Segal 2007, 15) in that they deny interrelatedness. Because dominant breast cancer narratives deny the fact that breast cancer is a "disease of populations" (Segal 2007, 8), that we are all "containers for environmental carcinogens" (Segal 2007, 14) and, by focusing on individual "battles" and individual "triumphs" they distract us by calling for a cure, rather than questioning the cause.

So let's call this a resistance narrative, a "renegade cancer story" (Segal 2007, 3), one that foregrounds and interrogates cancer as both characteristic of the anthropocene, and cancer treatment as a radical opportunity to come face to face with transcorporeality, that "movement across bodies" which emphasises the extent to which the substance of the human is ultimately inseparable from "the environment" (Neimanis and Walker 2013, 563).

At the time I was diagnosed, myself, my partner and our 2 kids (7 and 4) lived in a 26 square metre strawbale tinyhouse that we'd built ourselves. We had no running water other than the tap that came directly off our rainwater tank, offgrid solar power, an outdoors camp kitchen and a composting humanure toilet. Bathing

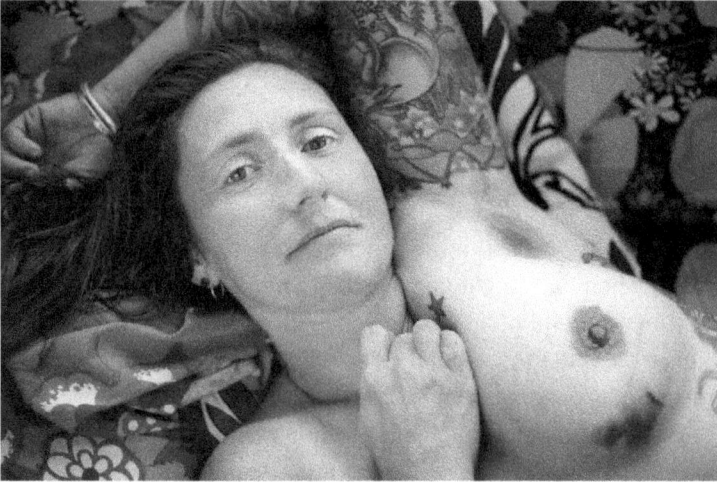

Figure 1. Biopsy.

involved collecting wood and lighting a fire underneath an old metal bathtub, which we filled using a hose. We were also running a pastured poultry business, supplying pasture-raised chicken to around 100 local families, and we ran a co-operative, community abattoir, where we worked, in addition to our off-farm jobs. For us, the hashtag #outsideeveryday was no fucking joke.

Our lifestyle profoundly complicated the 'flush it away' mentality that accompanies breast cancer treatment regimes, which insist on flushing/covering/disguising the hallmarks of cancer and its treatments. Breast cancer treatment also emphasises isolation, discretion and exclusion, where immune systems are compromised to nothing, and excreta is so toxic it must be flushed twice. For me, living as I was with a waterless composting toilet, this meant shitting in a deep hole in the middle of a paddock, away from tall trees. It was the middle of winter.

To be off grid – solely dependent upon your ability to read and participate in and work with the 'weather' is to be plugged into ecosystems, to become a finely attuned weatherbody, acutely conscious of ingress/egress of water/solar energy/'wastes'.

To be a small farmer – giving and taking life for the sustenance of a community, having the health and wellbeing of 600+ creatures under your care, managing those animals in a way

Annie Werner

that is ethical and regenerative – is to become finely attuned to nutrition/seasonal cycles/life and death/ecosystems/'weather'.

Our status as off grid small farmers solidified (or, as Astrida may suggest - liquefied) our status as transcorporeal weatherbodies.

Add cancer treatment into the mix – an opened and opening body, parts removed, highly toxic chemicals injected by the litre on

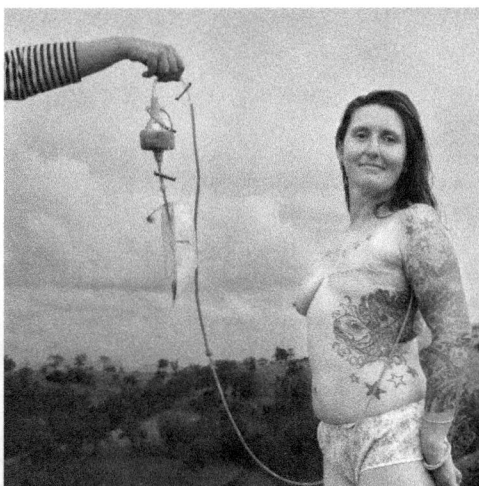

Figure 2. Drain.

a regular basis, bone marrow stimulants, steroids and antihistamines to trick my heart into not shutting down in protest against the chemo drugs, hormones disrupted/suppressed, bodily fluids extracted/drained/spontaneously and uncontrollably evacuated - and you have a peculiarly viscerally contemplative experience of weathering, illness, observing disease and its strange yet central position within the Anthropocene.

As I shat in my paddock-hole, I came face-to-face, body-to-body, with a version of Astrida Neimanis and Rachel Loewen Walker's formulation of weathering: "a logic, a way of being/becoming, or a mode of affecting and differentiating that brings humans into relation with more-than-human weather" (Neimanis and Walker 2013, 560). Just as they suggest understanding "climate change and human bodies as partaking in a common space, a conjoined time, a mutual worlding that we call weathering" (Neimanis and Walker 2013, 560) so too have I come to understand my experience of weathering cancer treatment whilst physically living the weather as an opportunity to understand material intersubjectivity.

In other words, cancer treatment presents an extreme foregrounding of transcorporality-in-action.

Figure 3. Dunny.

Discrete individualism, like normative, feminine behaviours and bodies, is obliterated by cancer treatment, which is why so much is invested in breast cancer narratives telling the 'right' kind of story, and maintaining the 'right' kind of bodies.

When I was diagnosed:

"You have extensive DCIS [baby breast cancer] and 2 aggressive cancers so you'll need a full mastectomy but don't worry you can have a reconstruction" – Dr Collins

The pathological reality of an extremely aggressive cancer in my body becomes, with not even a comma to acknowledge that this thing could actually kill me, a problem of normative gendered bodies. A problem to be solved, disguised, or covered. Visibility – of illness, of baldness, of booblessness – is problematic, disruptive to the dominant narratives that "tacitly (and sometimes not so tacitly) imply that the way to prevent the disease is to follow dominant codes of femininity" (Yadlon 1997, 648).

The lady in the chemo video told me that it was OK if I didn't feel like cooking dinner for my husband while I was having chemo. But that I should just get up off the couch, put a dressing gown on, and microwave something for him.

Annie Werner

Figure 4. Tiny House.

Meanwhile, down on the farm, I wasn't allowed anywhere near our chickens because of my compromised immune system, so my partner was running the whole operation by herself.

The lady from the "look good feel better" program kept calling me, concerned at my lack of interest in the program, assuring me that if I just put on a wig and wore some make-up, I'd definitely start to feel better.

Meanwhile, I wanted people to see what was happening to me, to bear witness to the processes I was undergoing, to share my rage at a system that demands isolation and denies interconnectivity, which demand that in the face of profound opening, we cover up and soldier on.

But how do we embody resistance and acknowledge and proclaim the transcorporeal truth? How do we brandish the inherent queerness of the post-breast-cancer body rather than deny and efface it?

I decided on an enormous chest tattoo. Apt, as well, because of the tattoo's cultural relationship with not-cohesive-or-sealed human bodies as signifiers of resistant ideology. Unfortunately for me, our health-care system (which I am grateful for, whilst also critical of) funds only socially sanctioned female bodies.

Figure 2. Drain.

So flat chested heavily tattooed bodies are off the agenda. Why is that?

The paranoid in me can't help but think that it's because post breast cancer bodies – weathered by surgeries and hair loss, weight loss and weight gain, and hormonal disruption are inherently queer, and, let's face it, we have a fairly well-pronounced cultural investment in heteronormative, gender-binarised bodies. What else could explain the overwhelming investment in keeping women's bodies looking 'feminine'?

So while the government would have paid for a boob job, I looked to my community and crowd-funded my dream chest.

The campaign was an opportunity to talk about different bodies, and our cultural investment in just one kind of body as being 'right' and 'desirable' and 'publicly fundable' and 'healthy'.

Because my body isn't any of these things. It isn't even mine. What it is is an opportunity for re-storying the narratives that seek to silence resistance and interrogation.

Works Cited

Neimanis, Astrida, and Rachel Loewen Walker. (2013). "Weathering: Climate Change and the 'Thick Time' of Transcorporeality." *HYPATIA-A Journal of Feminist Philosophy* 29(3), 558–575.

Segal, Judy Z. (2007). "Breast Cancer Narratives as Public Rhetoric: Genre Itself and the Maintenance of Ignorance." *Linguistics & the Human Sciences* 3(1) (April), 3–23.

Yadlon, Susan. (1997). "Skinny Women and Good Mothers: The Rhetoric of Risk, Control, and Culpability in the Production of Knowledge about Breast Cancer." *Feminist Studies* 23(3), 645–77.

Annie Werner

20 Weathering the Anthropocene at the End of the River: Thinking with Brine Shrimp in the Coorong, South Australia

Emily O'Gorman

Julie and I walked carefully along the stark white sand of the banks of the Coorong.[1] I was undertaking an interview for research on histories of wetlands in the Murray-Darling Basin. Julie is a long-time resident of a small settlement located about a third of the way south from the mouth of the Murray River, along the Coorong lagoon in South Australia. This lagoon is one of Australia's icon sites for the Living Murray initiative and listed on the Ramsar Convention for Wetlands of International Importance, known particularly for its birdlife (Murray-Darling Basin Authority; Ramsar Convention on Wetlands for International Importance; Kluske 1991 ,1-6; Jeffery 2001 , 29–30). It was summer and the water was low, exposing a wide shoreline with such a small incline that it looked almost flat; a sign of the shallowness of this part of the lagoon. In the distance, across the water, were 'The Hummocks', the sand dunes of Younghusband Peninsula, Karangk in the local Aboriginal languages of the Tanganekald or Tanganalun (Jeffery 2001, 29-31; Clarke 1994, 75-81). This peninsula was the setting of Colin Thiele's novel *Storm Boy*, a coming of age story that centres on the friendship between a boy and a pelican, that takes place against a national context of the Aboriginal land rights and environment movements of the 1960s. From the opposite shore and half a century later, we find ourselves at another, related, possible turning point in the Anthropocene.

From the moment we stepped on to the sand, Julie told me to be careful, that the shore was slippery. I began slowly, warily, but found the sand was firm and had a rough friction. I started to walk more confidently. We discussed the changes Julie had seen on the Coorong over the last fifteen years. The most recent drought, the Millennium Drought, infused our discussion. It had lasted longer here than elsewhere, from at least 2000 to 2011.

Julie told me how the humans and non-humans reliant on the waters of the Coorong had suffered. Water managers had not let fresh water though the barrages, built in the 1930s to protect irrigation interests. This meant that the Coorong did not receive freshwater inflows and became, in places, saltier than sea water. The pelicans which now frequently caught our attention, had for a time stopped breeding on the nearby islands in the lagoon, and other birds had also stopped breeding here too, fish reduced in number, people left the area as some industries could not function without more freshwater.

Julie turned to positive changes since the drought broke. The shoreline was gradually being repopulated by *Rupia tuberosa*, an aquatic plant that provided food for many water birds. The pelicans were back. As we began to return to the grassy bank I suddenly slipped in the sand. Julie said "look, that's the briney shrimp". I looked where my shoe had scraped back what I now saw was just a thin layer of white sand. Underneath was what appeared to be black clay. This is what had been slippery. I asked Julie, "the black stuff, is... shrimp?". "Yes!". She explained that during the drought the water in the southern lagoon of the Coorong had reached a level so salty that large numbers of the dormant brine shrimp had hatched. Others had said that a reduction in the number of fish predators meant that the shrimp had thrived. The decayed bodies of the shrimp formed a layer of black matter. They had been there, waiting, for just the right conditions. So many hatched that Banded Stilts, birds that normally fed on these creatures after floods in ephemeral, arid lakes, descended on the area for a feeding frenzy ("Cry me a River"). Some, then, had flourished during the drought. Yet many people on the Coorong had seen this burst of life as the death knell for the wetland. Julie had not. Clearly, Julie explained, while this was in some ways an unusual event for the Coorong it must have happened before. Yet, there was something different about this drought too.

While Australia is, in the words of Dorothea Mackellar, a land of "droughts and flooding rains" – an observation that has come to shape Australian national identity – the Bureau of Meteorology

Emily O'Gorman

declared the Millennium Drought to have been linked to anthropocentric climate change (Mackellar 1988; Bureau of Meteorology 2015; Steffan 2015, 15-17). This, together with significant changes to the Murray River system from large dams and more intensive agriculture in the twentieth century, along with the diversion of local inflows into the southern lagoon, had opened up an uncertain future for many in the area. In light of expected permanent changes, how could these sorts of these events now be interpreted? Droughts and shrimp hatchings resonated with the deep rhythms of this continent, only relatively recently recognised in Western science. In the Anthropocene they take on a new significance; rendered both familiar and unfamiliar at the same time. The decomposed bodies of the shrimp that formed such a distinct black layer brought us into the multiple temporalities and scales of this continent's history of deep time and upstream-downstream Murray River politics, of international environmental conventions and local industry, of unexpected and expected consequences, of possible winners and losers in the Anthropocene (Chakrabarty 2009, 207-212; Neimanis et al. 2051, 67-68; van Dooren 2016, 193-195). The black layer may not last, but the shrimp will be in the Coorong lagoon, waiting, perhaps playing the long game in a new epoch (Zalasiewicz et al. 2011, 835-836).

Notes

1   Names have been changed in this essay to protect the identity of research participants.

Works Cited

Bureau of Meteorology, "Recent Rainfall, Drought and Southern Australia's Long-term Rainfall Decline." Australian Government, April 2015, retrieved from http://www.bom.gov.au/climate/updates/articles/a010-southern-rainfall-decline.shtml, accessed 17 January 2018.

Chakrabarty, Dipesh. (2009). "The Climate of History: Four Theses." *Critical Inquiry* 35(2), 197-222.

Clarke, Philip. (1994). "Contact, Conflict and Regeneration: Aboriginal Cultural Geography of the Lower Murray." PhD, University of Adelaide, South Australia.

"Cry Me a River." (2008). *Sydney Morning Herald*, 21 June, retrieved from http://www.smh.com.au/news/water-issues/cry-me-a-river/2008/06/20/1213770924236.html, accessed 16 January 2018.

Julie, (2017). "Interview." *The Coorong* (March).

Jeffery, Bill. (2001). "Cultural Contact Along the Coorong in South Australia." *AIMA Bulletin* 25, 29–38.

Kluske, J. (1991). "Coorong Park Notes." National Parks and Wildlife Service. Netley, South Australia.

Mackellar, Dorothea (1988). *My Country*. Illustrated by Andrew McLean. Frenchs Forest, NSW: Child & Associates. Originally published 1908.

Murray-Darling Basin Authority. (n.d.). "The Living Murray program." Retrieved from https://www.mdba.gov.au/managing-water/environmental-water/delivering-environmental-water/living-murray-program, accessed 16 January 2018.

Neimanis, Astrida, Cecilia Åsberg, and Johan Hedrén. (2015). "Four Problems, Four Directions for Environmental Humanities: Toward Critical Posthumanities for the Anthropocene." *Ethics & the Environment* 20(1), 67-97.

Ramsar Convention on Wetlands for International Importance. (1998). "Information Sheet on Ramsar Wetlands: The Coorong, and Lakes Alexandrina and Albert."

Steffan, Will. (2015). "Thirsty Country: Climate Change and Drought in Australia." Climate Council of Australia.

Thiele, Colin. (1964). *Storm Boy*. Rigby: Adelaide.

van Dooren, Thom. (2016). "The Unwelcome Crows: Hospitality in the Anthropocene." *Angelaki* 21, 193-212.

Zalasiewicz, Jan, Mark Williams, Alan Haywood, and Michael Ellis. (2011). "The Anthropocene: A New Epoch of Geological Time?" *Philosophical Transactions of the Royal Society A: Mathematical, Physical and Engineering Sciences* 369, 835-841.

21 Jolts from the Geo-Climes

Wee Jasper Bush Salon

Abstract

The naming of the Anthropocene as a new epoch in which humans have become a geological force is sparking renewed interest in the geologic. At the same time, this paradoxical naming risks reinvigorating the conceits of human exceptionalism. In this hack we embrace the Anthropocene's call to the geologic while resisting the exceptionalisms of late Holocene humanism. We do this by thinking with the geo-climes of a Devonian limestone valley. The mind-bending temporalities, materialities, and geomorphic forces that form and weather this valley jolt us into recalibrating our all-too-human agentic scalar sensibilities.

Jolt #1

The almighty jolt and single cracking explosion comes completely out of the blue. It feels like the mountain has just been blown up. The jolt pushes the air out of our lungs. It triggers clouds of screeching birds to rise up out the valley. An eerie, still silence descends, as if nothing had happened. Consulting the Geoscience website, we find that it was a magnitude 3.7 earthquake, 4km deep and just 800 meters from our settlement (see Figure 1).

This recent earthquake was just a blip in the seismic history of this rift valley, which is slowly pulling apart. As the geologists tell it, the rift was formed by volcanic eruptions more than 400 million years ago, followed by a series of major convulsive lifts. The lifts exposed the sedimented strata of a calcified seabed laid down in the Devonian 'Age of Fishes'. They literally turned the ancient layered seabed on its side. Three hundred and forty million weathering years later, these prominent limestone synclines still traverse the landscape.[1] Life in the valley is historically and genealogically contingent upon the geo-bio-formations of its primordial past.[2] New life continually emerges from its mineralized corporeal remains. Kurrajong trees and brittle moss grow out of the rocky limestone outcrops and micro bats emerge from the depths of its caves (see Figure 2).

It's bat-counting season – late Autumn - the time when the scientists come to survey the endangered eastern bent-wing bats living in the 'maternity cave' down the road. Every spring, thousands of pregnant bats migrate to this cave to give birth to their pups and raise them over summer. The expanded colony leaves for the coast when winter sets in. The scientists conduct a nightly vigil at the cave entrance. They wait to count the bats as they fly out to feed. They used to enlist torch-wielding local volunteers to help them estimate the numbers. This year they have new technologies. They electronically count 39,000 bats with a thermal video camera and map their flight paths with Nasser missile tracking software[3] (see Figure 3).

The valley is renowned for its fossiliferous limestone outcrops. Paleontologists estimate that the perfectly preserved coral, trilobite, mollusc and lungfish fossils embedded in the limestone are 400 million years old.[4] They're from an era before plants and animals existed on land. And yet these other-worldy marine fossils are so commonplace. They're scattered everywhere. The deep time narratives are hard to reconcile with the fossils' everyday material presence. Other fossils have been found in the underground caves. These include 50,000-year-old calcified bone fragments from extinct marsupial mega fauna - the giant ancestors of the wombats that flourish in the valley today. These fossils come from a time that corresponds with human arrival in this place. This is much easier to grasp. The fossils remind us of the finitude of *all* species and prompt us to consider the future fossilization of our own.[5]

Jolt #2

Dry heat is pulsing through the long yellow grasses when we set off on the fossil tour. We head for a series of folded limestone ridges that wind down to the river. In the distance, the water looks alluringly cool. As we step onto the first line of exposed rocks, the tour-guide remarks: 'In that one step you just traversed 40,000 years.' We all look down at our feet and mentally measure them against the parallel strata that stretch out ahead at regular intervals. It's hard to comprehend. If one step equals 40,000 years, how many years of sedimented geological history lie in this strata sequence? How are our own steps being folded into the strata of this place (see Figure 4)?

Ever since its seismic formation, the riverine landscape has been continuously shape-shifted, weathered and eroded by a constellating assemblage of powerful forces. Recent human interventions have also made their mark. Early in the 20th century, building began on Australia's first major concrete-walled dam[6] just to the north of the valley, where rivers converge. It was purposed for irrigation and hydroelectricity, celebrated as a modern geo-engineering feat and took two decades to complete. It was also destined for obsolescence. The dam wall has twice threatened to collapse in major flooding events, requiring two substantial structural rebuilds in the last 50 years.. When the dam is full, the waters back up into the valley. They turn the river into a lake - submerging and killing trees, depositing silt and reshaping the valley floor. But not all of the shape-shifting action is in full display on the surface and so short-lived. As in all limestone karst country – millions and millions of years of steadily dripping, seeping groundwater is the critical weathering agent. Underground water moves down the fault line, connecting the higher altitude alpine karst systems to this valley. Carbonic acid in the water dissolves the soluble limestone bedrock, carving out a labyrinth of subterranean aquifer systems[7] (see Figure 5).

Jolt #3

It's hard to find a track through the waist high grasses and thistles. We pick our way gingerly, trying to avoid being scratched. Suddenly, we're standing unnervingly close to the edge of a dark abyss, about a metre wide. A sinkhole! How exciting, and how sobering. It's a miracle we didn't fall in! We wonder how deep it is, still coming to terms with our near miss. We lie on our tummies and edge closer to peer down to the bottom. We can't see any further than the first few metres of rocky wall. A local subsequently tells us that this particular sinkhole drops straight down about 40 ft. It links into an extensive cave system underneath the hill (see Figure 6).

Geologic Reflections

Being in the valley animates the sheer corporeality of the geologic, and stretches our imaginings of 'spacetimemattering'[8]. When we think with the mind-bending temporalities, materialities, and geomorphic forces that form and weather this landscape, we are jolted out of our human agentic/scalar sensibilities – and beyond the contractions of the Anthropocene.

Paradoxically, this same sense of the valley's inhuman scale prompts us to resort to the speculative algorithms of the geosciences. We find ourselves counting along - implicated in science's decidedly queer fetish for quantifying everything in the quest for certitude. But it's neither the lofty conceits of numerical abstraction, nor a blind faith in the technologies of measurement that impress us. It's the water-weathered rocks that transect and honeycomb the landscape, that encapsulate and issue life, which imprint themselves upon us. They remind us that we are just one ephemeral fold, destined to be fossilized, within the stratigraphy of the valley[9].

Figure 1. Limestone synclines traverse the landscape
Photo by Pam Rooney.

Figure 2. Kurrajong trees grow on rocky limestone outcrops.
Photo by Affrica Taylor.

Figure 3. Devonian fossils. Photo by Tonya Rooney.

Figure 4. Dam waters back up into the valley. Photo by Affrica Taylor.

Figure 5. Deep Sinkhole. Photo by Tonya Rooney.

Figure 6. The geologic stretches our scalar imaginary. Photo by Tonya Rooney.

The Wee Jasper Bush Salon is a loose feminist collective, which gathers irregularly to think, write, walk, swim, bird-watch, craft, create with/in the Wee Jasper valley, in the NSW southern tablelands. Its name is a nod towards the traditions of the European salons of the 18th and 19th century that fostered women's contributions to intellectual and cultural life. Members of the bush salon are associated with the feminist environmental humanities and experiment with creative and inclusive more-than-human methods. All of their activities are generated in collaboration with the valley's riparian geo/bio communities. Corresponding authors Affrica Taylor (University of Canberra) and Tonya Rooney (Australian Catholic University)

Notes

1   Detailed information about the geological history of the Wee Jasper valley can be found in Geological Society of Australia (ACT Division) *A Geological Guide to the Canberra Region and Namadgi National Park*, compiled by D.M. Finlayson (Canberra: Geological Society of Australia, 2008).

2   In their editorial introduction to a special issue of *Theory, Culture and Society*, called 'Geosocial Formations and the Anthropocene', Nigel Clark and Kathryn Yusoff (2017) warn against the premise of autonomous human geologic agency that can be easily inferred by the naming of the Anthropocene. They remind us that anthropogenic geological agency is neither 'new' nor inherently ours - it is an unfolding 'geosocial forma-tion', that comes from the earth itself. By raising questions such as: 'With what specific geological processes or properties have different social actors joined forces in order to acquire their geologic agency?'; and 'What manner of planet is this that gives rise to beings such as us in the first place? (p.5), they per-formatively entreat us to put 'social thought into an explicit, sustained and speculative interchange with its terrestrial ori-gins' (p.20). This is exactly what we are setting out to do as we think with the geo-climes of the Wee Jasper valley.

3   A rationale for this particular micro-bat research is presented in the online blog 'Going batty for the eastern bent-wing micro-bats' written by ANU students (April 21, 2015). The block offers background information to the research and includes personal anecdotes about and photographs of a research field trip to the Wee Jasper cave site. It can be accessed at: https://biodi-versityconservationblog.wordpress.com/2015/04/21/going-bat-ty-for-eastern-bent-wing-micro-bats/ . In another online post-ing, 'Thermal images and missile technology track microbat

colonies in NSW', Adrienne Francis (nd) elaborates on the new digital technologies of this research project and provides some amazing close up photographs of micro-bat colonies within the caves. Her posting can be accessed at: http://www.weejasper-caves.com/bats-thermal-imaging.html.

4   For further information about the fossils in the Wee Jasper val-ley, see 'Geological sites of NSW: Wee Jasper Caves and Fossils' (nd) http://www.geomaps.com.au/scripts/weejaspercaves.php. This site draws some of information from Ian Cathles, a local Wee Jasper landowner who has worked closely with paleon-tologists from the ANU for many years. Cathles is the local fossil expert and conducts fossil tours on his property in the valley. For more information about these tours and for photo-graphs of the fossils, see the 'Fossils' page of the Cooradigbee Homestead promotional website: http://www.weejasper.com.au/Fossils.html

5   In her article 'Geological subjects: Nonhuman origins, geo-morphic aesthetics and the art of becoming *in*human', Kathryn Yusoff (2015) reminds us that our species' origins and fates extend far beyond human temporalities and biological ma-terialities. She makes this point in order to counter the Anthropocene's narrative impulse to myopically re-iterate an exclusively human story, or what she describes, in more geomorphic terms, as the 'temporal and material contrac-tions of the Anthropocene' (p.383). Yusoff (2016) extrapolates on this point in 'Anthropogenesis: Origins and Endings in the Anthropocene', where she surmises that 'the Anthropocene has made man an end and origin in himself' (p.11). She argues that the notion of the Anthropocene deprives us of 'an outside to human time', because it effectively removes an apprecia-tion of the significance of deep time - the necessary 'ground and measure against which human finitude is exposed' (p.11). In particular, our fixation upon the Anthropocene, as the new and current Age of Man, obfuscates our 'energy debit' from the Carboniforous period (pp.11-12). Axiomatic to Yusoff's argu-ment, is an understanding that human life on earth is both relatively recent and contingent upon the vast geological epochs that came before us. As she stresses, our lives de-pend upon harnessing the energy of fossil fuels laid down in the Carboniferous period. This infers that our lives are inter-corporeally enmeshed with carbon fossils, literally composed by their 'antecedent materiality' (p. 26), and also awaiting transformation into a similar form of future materiality in our inevitable trajectory towards 'human-as-fossil-to-come' (p. 10).

6   The Water NSW website has a dedicated page to the dam to which we are referring. It is called 'Burrinjuck Dam: NSW's First Major Irrigation Dam' and includes maps and photographs, a history of the dam's construction, lots of factual information, as well as information for recreational visitors. It can be accessed at: http://www.waternsw.com.au/supply/visit/burrinjuck-dam

7   As the title of the website signals, the Burrinjuck dam was one of Australia's earliest large-scale hydro-engineering projects. The original grandiose early 20th century vision for the dam had all the hallmarks of modernity's blind faith in the geotechnical sciences to re-engineer 'nature' in order to reconstruct an 'improved' version of it. Researching the fraught history of the dam's construction, and witnessing first hand the ecological legacies it has left behind in the Wee Jasper valley, we are reminded of the futility of resorting to yet another geo-engineering 'fix' in response to the cascade of anthropogenic environmental disasters that characterise the Anthropocene. Clark and Yusoff (2017) articulate our skepticism when they comment: '… the unintended consequences of modernization have themselves been so widely experienced and so thoroughly thematized throughout the 20th century that the idea of the social reconstruction of the physical world going awry now seems almost routine. Is there anyone left on earth who actually believes geoengineering would go according to plan, should it come to that? (p.9).

8   Further information about the geo-historical formation and features of Wee Jasper's karst landscape and systems can be found in J.N. Jennings and J.A. Mabbutt (Eds) *Landform Studies from Australia and New Guinea*, Canberra: ANU Press, 1970.

9   We borrow Karen Barad's (2011) notion of 'spacetimemattering' to encapsulate the imbroglio of temporalities, materialities, and geomorphic forces that materialise this valley. Barad uses it to interrupt the binary logic of cause and effect, which assumes that pre-existing discrete entities act upon each other within linear time and in Euclidian space. Barad counter-theorises that phenomena (not separate and coherent entities) are the product of space/time/matter relations (or intra-actions). Moreover, they are produced by an emergent process that is simultaneously entangled and differentiating. As she posits in her 2010 'Quantum entanglements' article '… differentiating is a material act that is not about separation, but on the contrary about making connections and commitments …' (p.262). She also proposes that agency, along with emerging phenomena, is a relational effect.

10   Although we can never be entirely outside of the western sci-
     entific discourses we inhabit, we are nevertheless motivated by
     feminists such as Donna Haraway, (2016) and Anna Tsing (2015)
     who are taking the declaration of the Anthropocene as a figure
     signalling the inextricable enmeshment of natural and cultural
     worlds, and using it as an added incentive to experiment with
     collective more-than-human modes of thinking, practising and
     re-making worlds together. We take this moment as a bound-
     ary threshold, a time to adopt an ethics that seeks connection
     rather than separation and to redouble our efforts to learn
     from what is already going on in the world around us (Gibson,
     Rose & Fincher, 2015). Or, to use a lexicon that is more in keep-
     ing with the geo-spatial perspectives invoked by our relation-
     ship with the Wee Jasper valley, we can use 'the ecological-geo-
     climatic predicament' we face at this boundary threshold, to
     'prompt an especially intensive quest for new ways of inhabit-
     ing strata, of tapping terrestrial flows, of probing geomorphic
     possibility' (Clark and Yusoff, 2017, p.19).

Works Cited

Barad, K. (2010). "Quantum Entanglements and Hauntalogical
     Relations of Inheritance: Dis/continuities, Space/Time Unfoldings
     and Justice to Come." *Derrida Today* 3(2), 240-268.

Barad, K. (2011). "Nature's Queer Performativity." *Qui Parle: Critical
     Humanities and Social Sciences* 19(2), 121-152.

Biodiversity Conservation. (2015) ."Going batty for the
     eastern bent-wing micro-bats." Online blog written
     by ANU students, April 21, 2015. Available at: https://
     biodiversityconservationblog.wordpress.com/2015/04/21/
     going-batty-for-eastern-bent-wing-micro-bats/

Clark, N. and Yusoff, K. (2017). "Geosocial Formations and the
     Anthropocene." *Theory, Culture, Society* 34(2-3), 3-23.

Cooradigbee Homestead. (n.d.). "Fossils." Available at: http://www.
     weejasper.com.au/Fossils.html

Francis, A. (n.d). "Thermal Images and Missile Technology
     Track Microbat Colonies in NSW'. Available at: http://www.
     weejaspercaves.com/bats-thermal-imaging.html

Geological Society of Australia (ACT Division). (2008). *A Geological Guide to the Canberra Region and Namadgi National Park.* Compiled by D.M. Finlayson. Canberra: Geological Society of Australia.

Geological sites of NSW. (n.d.). "Wee Jasper Caves and Fossils." Available at: http://www.geomaps.com.au/scripts/ weejaspercaves.php .

Gibson, K., D. B. Rose, and R. Fincher (eds.) (2015). *Manifesto for Living in the Anthropocene.* New York: Punctum Books.

Grosz, E., Yusoff, K. and Clark, N. (2017). "An interview with Elizabeth Grosz: Geopower, Inhumanism and the Biopolitical." *Theory, Culture & Society,* 34 (2-3), 129-146.

Haraway, D. (2016). *Staying with the Trouble: Making Kin in the Chthulucene.* Durham: Duke University Press.

Jennings, J.N. and Mabbutt, J.A. (eds). (1970). *Landform Studies from Australia and New Guinea.* Canberra: ANU Press.

Tsing, A. (2015). *The Mushroom at the End of the World: On the Possibility of Life in the Capitalist Ruins.* Princeton NJ: Princeton University Press.

Water NSW. (n.d.). "Burrinjuck Dam: NSW's first major irrigation dam." Available at: http://www.waternsw.com.au/supply/visit/ burrinjuck-dam

Yusoff, K. (2015). "Geological Subjects: Nonhuman Origins, Geomorphic Aesthetics and the Art of Becoming *In*human." *Cultural Geography* 22(3), 383-407.

Yusoff, K. (2016). 'Anthropogenesis: Origins and Endings in the Anthropocene." *Theory, Culture & Society* 33(2), 3-28.

22 A Parent and Child Talk about the Weather

Abby Mellick Lopes and Louise Crabtree-Hayes

The weather was always a conversation starter, a way to deal with awkward silences and discomfort by turning to a shared background condition. But it also *declared* awkwardness and discomfort and an appropriate distance — the weather was rarely a topic of substance or intimacy. The conversation about the weather is however, changing.

Lately, weather talk has been taken out of the everyday and into the domain of urban design and planning, politics and political commentary where it layers over and hovers above people and how we live. Welcome to the world of strategies and standards, indicators and measures and visions of smart and resilient future cities able to adaptively withstand the Anthropocene. But what about the sweltering hot boxes of today (which are still being built) and the weather imposed on those of us living in them? Our hack seeks to bring talk about the weather back down to earth, into the house and under the table, in fact. The conversation between a parent and a child uncovers sensorial and bodily concerns about the weather inscribed in practice memories, pleasures and pains, dreams, fears and desires. At points, the conversation taps into latent knowledge that situates parent and child in an intergenerational and cultural field. As she gets more comfortable, the child starts to pick up cultural static and is at first confused (*how did I know that?*), but as the conversation progresses she becomes more assured of and confident in the latent knowledge she is channelling, which points to the capacities the two share and the collective memory they participate in. She tries to get the parent to see that. There's a lot to say — not that a parent always listens.

The following short scene was performed as part of Hacking the Anthropocene and tells of the experiences of people living in Penrith, Sydney who spoke to us about how they cope (or not) with long hot summers (see Mellick Lopes et al.). We discovered a wealth of practical and latent knowledge and experiences amongst residents, as well as creative ideas and aspirations for a cooler and more comfortable future. Alongside these lived and remembered knowledges, formal policy approaches to cooling struggled to gain traction amongst communities and residents, such that policymakers and the public were often speaking across or alongside each other, with little shared language or knowledge. We feel this presents an opportunity for shared and two-way learning to develop cooling practices.

It is an extremely hot day. The parent is returning from a shopping trip; she's juggling shopping bags, a crying baby, and a stack of junk mail from the mailbox.

Parent: *Yuck. It must be 40 degrees out there! Geez I wish they'd fix the bus stop! Waiting in the blazing sun for the bus, without any water except those plastic bottles in vending machines. They've taken out all the bubblers. And where's the bloody shade gone? God, if Council hadn't ripped out all those trees we'd be better off!*

The parent gets the baby a bottle of water, puts her in a bassinet, wets a sheet and puts it over the table, sets up the fan in front of the sheet, and turns it on. The fan blows through the wet sheet, sending cold air under the table.

Abby Mellick Lopes and Louise Crabtree-Hayes

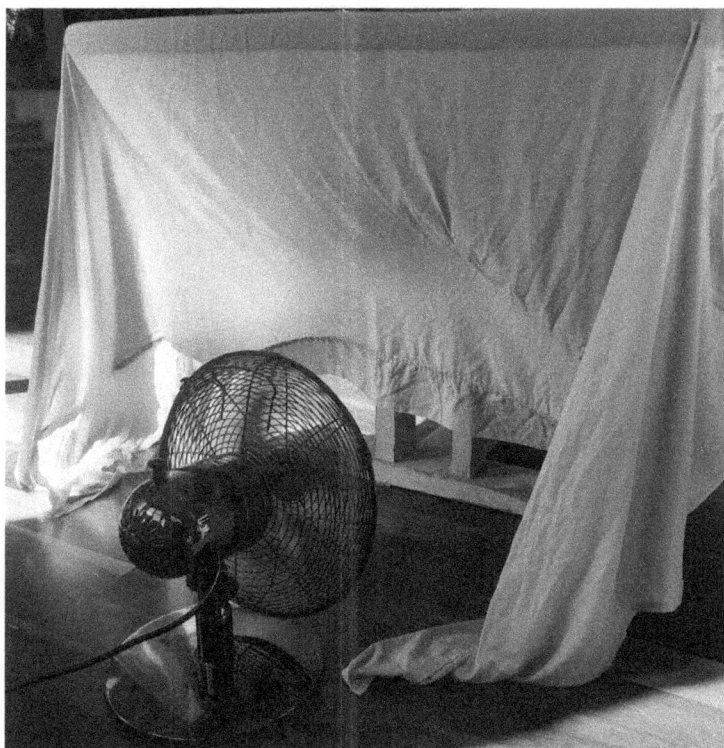

Parent: *Now you get under the table. Buggered if I can afford to fix the lousy air con they put in.*

Baby's internal voice, beneath the crying, which is starting to subside: *Mum, it's really good under here! You should come under here with me.*

Parent: *Now what's this pamphlet? It says something about a public meeting to talk about urban heat. Why do they want to talk about it? Why don't they just do something to make it easier for us? Bloody council!*

(Mum you are so clever, how did you know how to do this? It's so nice under here. Did grandma show you? Like she showed you how to fix the roof?)

Parent: *They say they want to hear my voice. Heard THAT before! Then they go and do the opposite! They say they want to hear from people who are "vulnerable" - female, pregnant with children - well I guess that's me.*

(...and how you made my room cooler by freezing water in cake tins and putting them near the fan? And putting wet flannels on my wrists and forehead? And rolling up a wet towel under the front door?)

Abby Mellick Lopes and Louise Crabtree-Hayes

They say it's because I'm hard to reach.

(Mum I don't think you are hard to reach!! I can hear you loud and clear. Are you listening to me though? Mum it's so nice under here, come under with me!)

Parent: *Bloody thick headed and tone deaf, is what they are. You kids can't even play in the park because we are still waiting for shade cloth and no bloody bubblers. Those bikes are rusting away outside.*

(Mum it's so cool under here, I'm going to need a blanket soon!)

Parent: *It's not rocket science – what are they going to do about this place? I'm renting, no bloody insulation and paper thin walls; I can hear every bloody fight they have next door. The owner won't listen. No garden, either. What are they going to do about that?? Those new developments look pretty much like more of the same, to me. They look like prison camps or substations!*

(Mum who made our house? Why don't THEY live in it?? But it's soo lovely under here, you are so clever – you made me a new cool room in our hotbox!)

Parent: *Hmmm it says here they want "a much greener, cooler more liveable and resilient place Western Sydney by 2026." 2026!! Apparently we've all got to be more 'resilient'.*

(Don't call ME resilient! Mum you sound so neoliberal when you say stuff like that! Oh wow – how do I know about the role of resilience in neoliberal discourse? I sure don't like how it smells.)

Parent: *When they say that they mean they want us to do everything ourselves. Well they've got to do stuff too!*

Abby Mellick Lopes and Louise Crabtree-Hayes

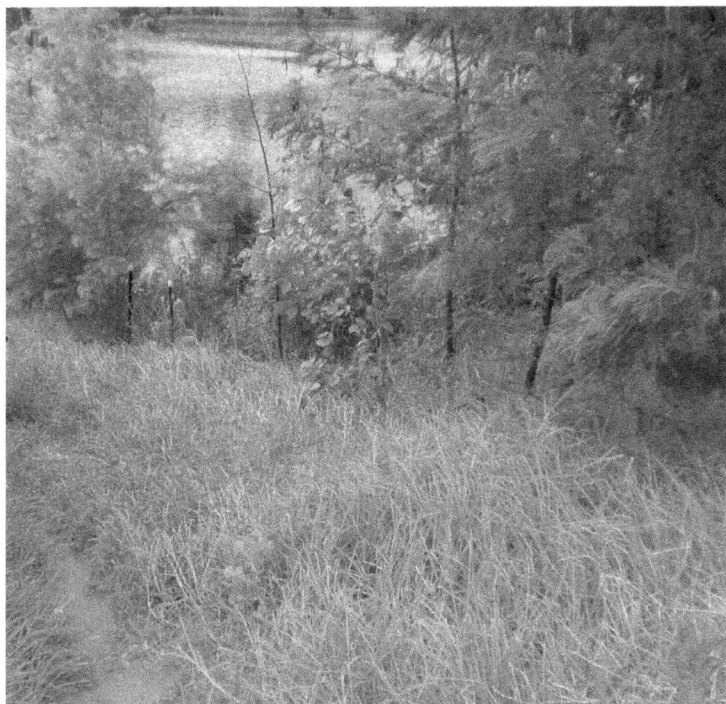

(We've been here a long time and I remember all sorts of stuff. I remember us being here for millennia. My body remembers this world. "We are the world"... hang on, why do I know that song? That's not one of yours... Where's all this knowledge and big words coming from? Being alive is really intense sometimes. Is this how collective memory works? Hey, mum, you should tap into this! You've got so much of it and probably know more about these big words than I do... Remember when you took me to the park near the river? It was nice lying under the trees looking up through the leaves and the breeze was coming off the river and we had a nice outside dinner – even if Dad was upset we had to wait for the barbie...

...Wouldn't it be good if the park was set up as an outdoor place to cook? We could get together with the other kids more and you could see your friends more, instead of once a week when the big yellow bus comes to our local park.

Mum we've got HEAPS to say at the meeting, we should go!!)

Parent: *It says they've got a new inclusive strategy they want to implement and they want to involve me in that and they're going to make a working party and a steering committee and have a new vision and new health policies about increasing our MVPA (that's moderate to vigorous physical activity)...*

Abby Mellick Lopes and Louise Crabtree-Hayes

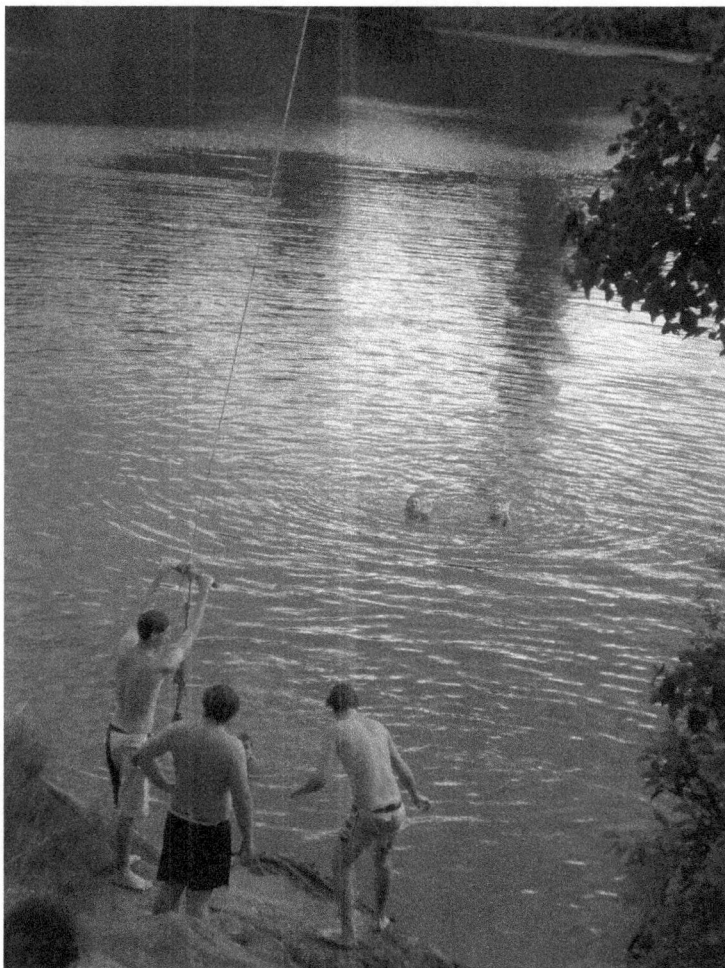

(Hm... MVPA... Mum's Very Practical Agency?? I like the fan and
sheet policy mum! We know more than them about living here.
What about all the stories you told me of when you were a kid
when you rode your bike down to go swimming in the river and
made a swing from the trees? Why can't we talk about that? Why
won't they let us swim in the fancy water fountain across the
road? We can just walk there, unlike the river. Why did they turn it
off? Mum we have to go to the meeting!)

Parent: *What was that? Did you say something? Blimey – I'm imagining the baby talking. Heat must be getting to me.*

(You haven't been listening have you? I said you know heaps and we should go to the meeting.)

Parent: *OK well I guess I'll go to the meeting if you come with me.* [Squats down, puts head around the sheet to talk to the baby] *You want to come to a meeting, bubby?*

(There you are Mum!! I'll come with you but only if you get under the table with me)

Parent: *OK then. Let's do this.* (joins baby under table)

From under table – *Oh wow. it IS nice under here!!*

(See, Mum? You really do know lots of stuff!!)

Acknowledgements

Images 1 to 9, Photography by Abby Mellick Lopes. Image 10, Photography by Helen Armstrong, reproduced with permission. Images 7-10 were taken during field research as part of the project: Zoe Sofoulis, Helen Armstrong, Michael Bounds, Abby Mellick Lopes and Tara Andrews. *Out & About in Penrith, Universal Design and Cultural Context: Accessibility, diversity and recreational space in Penrith.* Centre for Cultural Research, UWS with Penrith City Council, June 2008, www.penrithcity.nsw.gov.au/images/documents/building-development/planning-zoning/Out_About_Final_Report.pdf

Abby Mellick Lopes and Louise Crabtree-Hayes

Work Cited

Mellick Lopes, Abby, Gibson, Katherine, Crabtree, Louise, & Helen
    Armstrong. (2016). *Cooling the Commons Pilot Research Report.*
    Institute for Culture and Society, Western Sydney University,
    October, available at www.westernsydney.edu.au/__data/assets/
    pdf_file/0020/1161470/cooling-the-commons-report.pdf

23 Weathering Paperfare in Contemporary Wars of Attrition

Tess Lea

Weathering
Wea|ther
/ˈwɛðɚ/
VERB

1. Wear away or change the appearance or texture (of something) by long exposure to the atmosphere: "his skin was weathered almost black by his long outdoor life"

2. *Synonyms:* weather-beaten * eroded * worn * disintegrating (Of a ship) come safely through (a storm). "the sturdy boat had weathered the storm well"

3. Make (boards or tiles) overlap downwards to keep out the rain

4. Falconry (weathering) Allow a hawk to spend a period perched in the open air.

(Weathering definition, google.com)

A falcon *weathering* is not, as one might think, cleaving the open air, feathers fibrillating in infinite attunement with currents and drafts. It is a captured bird, kept in a mews, an enclosure to perch within that is partly permeable to daylight, as open as chicken mesh allows. The caged bird 'weathers' when it spends a period of its time roosting in unopen air. It is akin to a form of bureaucratic enclosure, this version of weathering (Lea 2012).

As an anthropologist, I study policy worlds, which are also race worlds and money worlds. Worlds which are embodied, where bodily freedoms are shaped and limited by the enclosures they are in. It is of utmost significance that policy bodies occupy coops comprising non-opening windows for weathering indoors

Figure 1. Weathering policy enclosures. Photo by Tess Lea.

bathed in semi-natural light, amid cubicles, carpets, swivel chairs and internet capacity, kitchens with hot water for tea and coffee coming from press-button taps, with warnings about fairies not being real so please clear away the dirty dishes.

Weathering also means to endure, to survive, to ride out, withstand, resist. And re-angled, it is to show the marks of these endurances, the traces that surviving and withstanding might leave on a body, be it rock or organ, the effects of time and events borne.

> The skin takes colours after middle age,
> An elbow flakes, one ankle always raw,
> A shoulder wart, sebaceous stains on backs.
> (Oliver 1986, 14)

It is with these different senses of weathering – of being enclosed, but allowed to feel a certain kind of freedom, however foreclosed; of enduring and showing the marks and scars of that survival – that I want to reference Australia's northern most capital, Darwin. I attend in particular to what we might extract as

Figure 2. Kakadu escarpment. Photo by Tess Lea and Cornel Ozies.

lessons from the north, as well as some anthropogenic conceits that we should not contentedly hack.

Darwin

There is so much to say about this little city, the least well known on the Australian national map – how it tilts at the elemental forces which continue to pound and harry its chosen location (Lea 2014). Here I will limit the ambit to three propositions. First, consideration of Darwin and what it has weathered lets us consider the weathering events yet to be endured elsewhere. While Darwin is a sporadic thought bubble in terms of national politics, it concentrates and gives warning of issues people elsewhere will increasingly confront, as we start weathering new weathers. Second, endurance is built into its curious name. Charles Darwin, master of calling attention to 'the imperceptible movements, modes of becoming, forms of change and evolutionary transformations' that he observed around him (Grosz 2011, 1), is named at this place of immanence, of resurrection and permeability. The rich variability of human and non-human life in and around Darwin, forces a pause to that stubborn and still-with-us popular and scholarly insistence that the social and political can be divorced from the more-than-human. Darwin is sculpted by

Tess Lea

its geolocation and human/non-human entanglements in every way imaginable. Finally, despite resisting the call to name itself after Anglo Celtic lords and politicians, it nonetheless represents ongoing occupation on Indigenous land. As the first place to withstand foreign contact, and the last place to endure sustained colonially-sponsored settlement, it vividly encompasses the intersection of contemporary settler colonial politics and what the Anishinaabe scholar Gerald Vizenor has called "survivance" (Vizenor 2009, 100). In his seminal model, "nature has no silence" (Vizenor 1994, 52). Survivance is the

> "state or condition," or "action," as in *continuance.* Survivance … is the action, condition, quality, and sentiments of the verb *survive*, "to remain alive or in existence," to outlive, persevere with a suffix of survivancy. (Vizenor 2009, 100)

In Australia, survivancy has always been about killing and fucking and loving, hating and cruelling, avoiding and partnering, thwarting and co-creating, narrating, simulating, haunting. We don't call the weathering of settler colonialism by these adjectives, but by policy epochs. First, invasion; then the killing times; the mission era and assimilation; self-determination and land rights. And now? Some call it neo-liberalism and catch far too much in that label. I will call it the era of paperfare (Lea et al. 2018) and slow death, meaning by this a new form of eroding Indigenous resistance executed through English-language legalisms, of wearing people down through extortionate encounters with infinite variations of administrative violence (see also Graeber 2012; Povinelli 2016; Grealy 2017).

Thinking about the slow death of battles fought through settler colonial paperwork, what are we asking Indigenous people to continually weather, whenever we gesture to their survivance as the answer to dominant societal anthropogenic nightmares?

But first, let's return to the place of elemental lessons: Darwin, in the north of Australia.

Weathering virtual futures

One Christmas Eve, when I was eight years old, the winds roared and a massive African tulip tree fell, thrown to the ground like a discarded toothpick from an insouciant giant's finger-flick. Then the roof came off my bedroom. The enclosure promised by this space of night-time cocoons, monsters and stories, lost its capacity to contain. I am not a falcon seeking to sail on winds. I wanted my pen to stay intact; and so I hung onto a piece of wall that fell on me as the roof took to the skies. I hung on grimly, permanently bending my ring finger and traumatising my right shoulder, now haunted by cyclone-gifted arthritis, as I tried to make a roof from the scrap left to me, until it too airlifted into the hurtling ribbons of that wild night sky.

Cyclone Tracy, December 24, 1974, destroyed 80 percent of all residences and turned all Darwin's people into refugees (Cunningham 2014).

Here is what else I learnt about Darwin as a place of elemental forces. This is the place of things to come. Its centrality to our future is not based on numbers. It is a small place, reckoned numerically. Around 140,000 people. Its future portents lie in its history of destruction. It has been smashed four times already in its short existence as a settlement: three times by cyclones, including that proper wild one called Tracy, and famously, by Japanese bombing attacks, sustained over an 18 month period in World War Two (Lockwood 1966). That it is serially rebuilt – against all logic – is harnessed as proof of the resilience of the people, of their ability to withstand the catastrophic, to weather disasters.

To a certain extent this is true. In the immediate aftermath of the wartime bombings and again after Cyclone Tracy, vigilante groups, including some military, contributed to the mayhem, looting what they could, shooting at what they shouldn't. Tales of reconstruction madness reveal town planning fiascos, led by too many men coming in from far afield to boss surviving locals around, then running out of expertise, commitment and easy money to see anything through. The processes for getting ideas approved were administratively brutal and badly botched

Tess Lea

by random regulations and arbitrary requirements. Insurance claims suspended people in loss-making limbos past the time of viable return, strangled by new stipulations and delayed paperwork. Restoration planning concepts were cruelled by committees with too many competing ideas and too much arrogance to parse through what, of the local architecture that had existed before, should be repeated as good design, given these had not survived aerial bombs or wild gales. (Think about it: If a semi-trailer can be lifted into the air, what hope the most well-designed house?)

While disaster may be part of Darwin's DNA, it demands perseverance to repeatedly resurrect from such ruins. Making things work for people who survive takes interminable public pressure and collective weathering. And here our first lessons. This was no once-in-a-lifetime storm (however formative Cyclone Tracy was for me), but a vision of shared futures, already thrumming in the past. Darwin is to be a city where temperatures will rise above 35C *265 days a year*, up from the current average of 11 days (Steffen et al. 2017, 78).

It will not be alone. All Australian heatwaves will start earlier in a season, and last longer. There will be longer lasting droughts; harsher fire weather across southern and eastern Australia; the storms will be more intense; rainfalls more relentless; and coastal flooding more frequent as broken reefs and high sea levels breach more fragile boundaries. And those warming oceans, those ones bleaching the Great Barrier Reef in multiple tragedies of the multispecies commons, will spur those winds into more destructive furies. Wild and beautiful and oh so deadly. Further, like coastal cities elsewhere, Darwin is sinking. The seas have been rising since the last Ice Age, creeping from the edge of the continental shelf back in, creating a delta where river valleys once were. Very little of Darwin is far above sea level as it is. And sea levels are rising there faster than anywhere else in the world, at 8.3mm per year (Terzon 2016). It is a city floating on ancient ridgelines that are slowly being sucked into seawater. Drowning, standing still.

Darwin as a collective virtual reality for those in other places is not just based on the spectre of rising waters and unbearable heat. It is based too, on the reasons for Darwin's continuous rebuilding. As poorly located as it might be as a city, it is an excellent site for deploying weaponry toward the arc of nations that Americans might choose to destroy, in other becomings that are just as present (Lea and Rollo 2016). Because of its geolocation, close to the Darwin is a defence garrison; and host to a rotating presence of American Marines as part of the United States' Asia-Pacific security architecture. As I have written elsewhere with Stuart Rollo

> The tactical value of Darwin rests in its proximity to the Straits of Malacca, the skinny stretch of water between Singapore, Malaysia and Indonesia. Only 2.7km at its narrowest point, the Straits are a well-known strategic chokepoint. If blocked, nearly half the world's shipping fleet would have to reroute through the Indonesian archipelago. As the shortest sea route between the Gulf countries and Asia, the Straits are also China's energy corridor—80 per cent of China's crude oil imports pass through the Straits. (Lea and Rollo 2016, 31)

By maintaining the capacity to interdict shipping through the Strait of Malacca, the United States holds a strong deterrent against any possible Chinese military action using Darwin as its launching pad. As a military outpost, Darwin thus has a reason for being; at least for now. Its military usefulness and entanglement in imminent trade and territory conflicts also reflect the imminence of conflicts to come from climate change and population mobility issues. Darwin may need to be raised, razed or relocated; the military will likely be part of that. This too is a potential condition of many shared futures.

Endurance/entanglement

Like Santa in 1974, Charles Darwin did not make it to Darwin. When the offer came to join the Beagle once more for its third and final circumnavigation, he could not bring himself to board ship. A rebellious stomach lurched into his nervous system. His first and now most famous trip around South America was meant to take two years, maximum. It took nearly five. And whenever he was at sea, Darwin fell sick to the motion.

Plymouth, England, December 27, 1831:

After months of delays, the Beagle finally departs: "The misery I endured from sea-sickness is far beyond what I ever guessed at" (American Museum of Natural History).

From Bahia, August 1836, reflecting on the idea of returning to South America for additional longitudinal measurements:

> This zig-zag manner of proceeding is very grievous...I loathe, I abhor the sea, & all ships which sail on it. Not even the thrill of geology makes up for the misery and vexation of spirit that comes with sea-sickness (American Mueseum of Natural History).

As Astrida Neimanis reminds us, thinking is embodied.

> A pressing thirst can similarly disorient the organizing project of our subject-selves. Thirst diffracts me, I lose my focus. I cannot concentrate on the words on the page, or keep my thoughts trained. My throat searches for some forgotten cache of saliva and the incessant attempts to swallow distract me. ('What did you say? What was that again?') (Neimanis 2016).

From all accounts Darwin was a pleasantly mannered man, but as a sailor he was all at sea, not good with hauling ropes, nor at reading the weather and watery swells; yet his vile liquid tempests let him prove his mettle in other ways. Vomiting, returning to his books, retching again, working harder, his cabin mates began to see something heroic, something valiant in his ability to weather, we might say. Thus it was that years later, on the ship's third journey, when these same cabin mates went ashore at a point along the Arafura Sea, searching for that mythical inland river to help loot and rearrange the Australian hinterland toward extraction industries and agriculture, they noted the interesting geological formations, weathered over eons, and thought of their old mate, Charles, naming 'the wide bays appearing' in his honour.

The rest of the place did not look so promising.

There was nothing of interest to recall our memories to this first visit to a new part of Australia, save a very large ants nest, measuring twenty feet in height. This object is always the first that presents itself whenever my thoughts wander to that locality (Stokes 1846).

Figure 3: Nothing of interest save an ant nest. Photo by Tess Lea.

Tropical places seem to push back harder than temperate ones, which is another lesson about weathering. Between its dramatic upheavals, Darwin is a patient settler adversary. One day you might push against wall cladding and have it vanish to powder, eaten hollow by termites, those far-from-dull cathedral makers. Water pushes into weaknesses in buildings shaken by storms then left porous by the baking of hot days and the slaking of monsoonal drenchings. There are times of the year where everything joins in struggle, when shoes left unworn renew their acquaintance with colourful old mates: green, grey and black moulds, tightening sinuses, binding heads, whirring histamines. Clothes dampen; skin sticks to the skin you're in. Cockroaches eat documents, etching nibble tracks and leaving stains from their pupae and shit. And then there are the deadly little female hunters, the mosquitoes.

Sickening populations with malaria and dengue fever, these 'single mothers' (Nading 2012) helped destroy the first four attempts at settling the northern coastline before Darwin became the resolute destination. Despite official rear-guard efforts to control their breeding grounds, with chemical poisoning of aquatic habitats and fogging (at first with dichlor odiphenyltrichloroethane, or DDT[1]), mosquitoes still swarm in

Tess Lea

the stifling periods between rains and king tides. Those military efforts which, in separate genealogies, yielded the techniques for killing mosquitoes *en masse*, also aided and abetted their breeding, carving nurseries in swamp craters blasted from bomb practice in the post war period. The craters filled with unexploded ordnance and larvae in brackish pools, a perfectly protected combination. Tackling these issues at the local level, through a more workable mix of co-existence (preventing suburbs encroaching too far into wetlands) and learn-from-error hydrology, like the resurrections of Darwin's built environment after each levelling, has in turn required steerage through the legal-bureaucratic labyrinths of still-colonial administration dealt from afar (Lea 2014, 83-91).

These long, tortuous, regulatory and protection battles lack joy. They cause stress, even for those paid professional wages to slog through. Another set of small lessons: the techno-scientific solutions served within the anthropogenic spectre offers collateral damages, written in sometimes invisible font. This should make critics more wary of our tacit desire for a sensible centre of governance, for the state to know best how to act, when we call for better policy and oversight. For Darwin also teaches about the endemic nature of administrative failing and the toll of these combats on people, places and other lives, measured in high turnover rates (Carson et al. 2010, 295-6), bodily chronicities, disease burdens and drug addictions (Zhao et al. 2016), and fast-paced mammalian extinctions (Woinarski et al. 2015).

Weathering paperfare

Being worn down, enduring, survivance. To conclude, let me attempt to bring these points together. Because Darwin is a place where the profit pursuits of settler colonialism are not yet exhausted, it is also where lessons on weathering the exhaustions of the policy shapeshifting that underwrites the race for what is left (cf. Klare 2012) are also more explicit. Settlers now want what they forced Aboriginal people to put up with, when barren lands were agricultural remainders, forcing new dispossessions in the present. Expelling people from land has many guises (Pasternak and Dafnos 2017, 739-750), including the crude form of the Northern Territory Emergency Response, aka 'the intervention' (Altman and Hinkson 2007).

The dramatic declaration of a national emergency in Northern Territory Indigenous communities in June 2007 was ostensibly triggered by the release of *Ampe Akelyernemane Meke Mekarle "Little Children are Sacred": Report of the Northern Territory Board of Inquiry into the Protection of Aboriginal Children from Sexual Abuse* (Wild and Anderson 2007). According to the report, 'rivers of grog [alcohol]', rampant child sexual abuse and organized paedophilia rings were destroying any capacity of Indigenous people to exercise normal function. Wild and Anderson's inquiry into sexual abuse had in turn been commissioned by the Northern Territory Government one year earlier, based on public outrage following a different kind of reporting: a television interview with Dr Nanette Rogers, an experienced Crown Prosecutor based in Alice Springs, a small service town in the middle of Australia, on the Australian Broadcasting Commission's current affairs program, Lateline. Dr Rogers detailed sickening cases of children suffering at the hands of their drunken and depraved family members, providing graphic details of babies raped so badly their genitals needed surgical repair; of a paralyzing malaise among all the groups that could possibly intervene; and a worrying lack of prosecutorial powers to do much to prevent it (Jones 2006). The prosecutor was overworn, at the end of her wits: she had to speak, she said; she could not hack it anymore (Australian Broadcasting Corporation 2006).

People were drafted into this response immediately. Retired doctors and locum nurses, new police and community development positions, new roles for Business Coordinators in each prescribed community, new money for staff and community housing, many meetings to attend. The Australian airline carrier, Qantas, put on additional scheduled flights to and from Darwin, enabling southerners to descend on a Monday and leave on a Friday, such was the travel demand. Within the bureaucracy, it was a time for making funding submissions to add capacity to existing data collections and develop new warehousing sites, in the name of being able to evaluate the impacts of all these new initiatives. The number of non-Indigenous people engaged to help Indigenous people swelled, inviting loud denunciations of its paternalistic mode, its deployment of the military, the magnified surveillance and policing systems, and the Intervention's recall of times-not-long past where children were spirited out of mothers' hands, when missions were sub-contracted by governments to deal with the collateral damage of feeding a new nation of dislocated people.

Bureaucracy as new form of letting live and letting die

Yet it is not the spectacle of the Intervention that I want to end on but the less dramatic ways in which the state intensified what I will call, dragging an environmental toxicity argument into the domain of paperwork, slow *administrative* violence (cf. Nixon 2011). I am thinking in particular here of my ongoing anthropological fieldwork, in which I have been tracking key Indigenous reformers who, as Haraway might say, have stayed with the trouble (Haraway 2010), not as a scholastic determination but as a decision with few alternatives.

A key thing to hold in mind: being officially *incorporated* in one way or another, as registered individuals or organisations, is the only way Indigenous people can legally receive money. Organisational forms have thus proliferated. Without mining (and even with mining) these are often organisations surviving on 'soft money'; which is to say, on the brokerage, translations and semiotic performances required for multiple grants, acquittals and client-patron impression management (Mosse and Lewis 2006; Michel and Taylor 2012). This concentrates a demand for bureaucratic writing, a mode of communicating which is inherently exclusionary (Mignolo 1992, 818-19, 824-25), demanding literacies in institutional English and a grasp of the abstractions of administrative concepts. What, after all, is a 'summary of key outcomes'? A business case? A financial statement? A productivity levy? An output-based acquittal? In turn Indigenous people often have to employ or collaborate with non-Indigenous people to access necessary bureau-strategic capital simply to co-exist (Batty 2005, 209).

But this is not the only, nor even major, entailment of contemporary administrative colonialism (Neu 2000, 268-70). For it is not simply paperwork over or about Indigenous people which encodes what happens to who, how, for what kind of money; but a new-old mode of draining life-worlds entirely legally, without visible violence or notable theft, via contracts, grants, regulations, negotiations, standards, accountabilities, enumeration and the avoidance, thwarting, attenuation, non-counting or perennial bastardisation of all of these mechanisms, *that people must now weather.* We might think about files, what is kept in and what is missing from them. Forms, and what they do and don't count. Regulations, and what they do and don't protect; a river perhaps, or a deregulated bank as one which directs financial regulations in its favour (Lea 2020).

Why do we need to think of administrivia and its latencies? Buried within our many critiques of anthropogenic apocalypse, in accounts of what *our* unchecked desire for bio-petro-fuelled existence has placed at risk, lie two key concepts:

1. Indigenous lifeworlds represent an alternative, an otherwise, that teaches us how to live more attuned to the non-human universe (Viveiros de Castro 2013; Hage 2015); and

2. The state needs to determine the policies and fund-ing inducements and fines to reroute our techno-capital regimes into eco-friendly, 'sustainable', modes and provide a decent blueprint for action.

Under the first move, Indigenous alternatives become, in Lucas Bessire's terms, "the primary inspiration for radical imaginaries of alternate modernities based on inverting Enlightenment divides between nature/culture or human/nonhuman" (Bessire 2014, 277). Idealised Indigenous people are positioned as mnemonics for our possible otherwise. But while the image might have mesmerising appeal, this actually inhabited space is not one of pristine harmonious forms but of survivance in a more embattled zone, where frontier violence executed through paperfare is right now being waged. Some of this paperfare, as my Darwin example sketched, is generic to surviving disasters and being administered by distant experts; but generic application does not mean equal distribution of entailments and harms. Under move two, whether we realise what we are asking for or not, from setting emission targets to protecting old growth forests to dealing with nuclear waste, sponsoring solar energy or the greater supply of public transport – beyond statelessness, which by definition such calls do not imagine – all require regulations, restrictions, government intervention and public investment, if they are to be contained, ameliorated, initiated, together with a mobilisation of technocratic legalities if they are to be held true.

Here is my point. This is already the space of the Indigenous otherwise. The environmental safeguards that are demanded by Indigenous people as their lands are pillaged in the race to serve our mineral/fuel/chemical fed dependencies on phones, planes and freighted food delivery systems, have to be fought for, in unequal battles where the multinational company can fill a boardroom with Queen's Counsel overnight, and the grassroots organisation faces the extortionate costs of facing Queen's Counsel with over-acquitted resources and single printers (Lea, et al. 2018). Safeguards exist and are only enforceable through advocacy, naming and shaming through the press, harrying of bureaucrats, thence onto the courts, through demands to make systems of accountability count, for lives to be counted in accountable ways. If you are sick, unemployed, impoverished, unable to travel, unable to print, then you depend on others even more; and maybe all you are seeking is a house with running water and a working toilet, because the mine has already shifted your river and the lead is already in your game.

To close the loop: if the resurrections of Darwin teach us anything, it is that vectors of disease, human-other entanglements, new inequalities laminating onto older ones,

Figure 4. Extractions. Photo by Tess Lea.

are scooping in the lives of the previously protected. That's us. Anything decent will have to be fought for, before, during, after, in both spectacular disasters and their corrosive quasi-event kin (Povinelli 2011, 13-14). To get better at anticipating this part of what will be weathered, we have to hack into the narrative conceits, the escape clauses in our critiques, where Indigenous epistemologies are pointed to as a wiser way of being in the world as we simultaneously call for ways to make 'the system' work better. Both gestures disregard the real time battles being waged as Indigenous people conduct the battles that are also ours, when climate forces unwanted levellings and new alliances. And we can prepare, for we are already (in) this system.

Notes

1   Mosquitoes everywhere have weathered these counter attacks, and developed enzymes to detoxify insecticides. The indiscriminate use of DDT in industrialised agriculture also accelerated a population of resistant mosquitoes. In Malaya, *kampong* dwellers accused the anti-malaria teams of making their roofs

fall down by the use of DDT; and resisted WHO-funded eradica-
tion campaigns. Why?

"The roofs were made of *attap* (palm fronds), and there was
an *attap*-devouring caterpillar that dwelt in the roof. In normal
conditions a parasitic wasp preyed on these pests and kept
their numbers down, but the wasps were highly sensitive to
DDT and the caterpillars were resistant. Consequently, when
the malaria workers sprayed the *kampongs*, the wasps died,
the caterpillars proliferated, and within a month all the roofs
came crashing down. After that, unsurprisingly, malaria workers
were no longer welcome." Desowitz (1991) 140.

Works Cited

Altman, J. and M. Hinkson, Eds. (2007). *Coercive Reconciliation:
Normalise, Stabilise, Exit Aboriginal Australia.* Melbourne, Arena
Publications.

American Museum of Natural History, http://www.amnh.org/
exhibitions/darwin/a-trip-around-the-world/a-five-year-
journey/, accessed 14 April 2018

Australian Broadcasting Corporation. (2006). "Crown Prosecutor
speaks out about abuse in Central Australia." *Lateline.* Australia,
Australian Broadcasting Corporation.

Batty, P. (2005). "Private Politics, Public Strategies: White Advisers
and their Aboriginal Subjects." *Oceania* 75(3), 209-221.

Bessire, L. (2014). "The Rise of Indigenous Hypermarginality: Native
Culture as a Neoliberal Politics of Life." *Current Anthropology*
55(3), 276-295.

Carson, D., D. Schmallegger, et al. (2010). "A City for the Temporary?
Political Economy and Urban Planning in Darwin, Australia."
Urban Policy and Research 28(3): 293-310.

Cunningham, S. (2014). *Warning: The Story of Cyclone Tracy.*
Melbourne, Text Publishing.

Desowitz, R. S. (1991). *The Malaria Capers: Tales of Parasites and
People.* New York and London, Norton.

Graeber, D. (2012). "Dead Zones of the Imagination: On Violence,
Bureaucracy and Interpretive Labour." *HAU: Journal of
Ethnographic Theory* 2(2), 102-128.

Grealy, L. (2017). "Paperless Arrests as Preventive Detention: Motion and Documentation in the Governance of Indigenous Peoples of Australia." *Sites: A Journal of Social Anthropology and Cultural Studies.*

Grosz, E. (2011). *Becoming Undone: Darwinian Reflections on Life, Politcs and Art.* Durham, Duke University Press.

Hage, G. (2015). A*lter-Politics: Critical Anthropology and the Radical Imagination.* Melbourne, Melbourne University Press.

Haraway, D. (2010). "When Species Meet: staying with the trouble." *Environment and Planning D: Society and Space* 28(1), 53-55.

Jones, T. (2006). "Crown Prosecutor Speaks Out About Abuse in Central Australia." *Lateline.* ABC Corporation, Australian Broadcasting Corporation.

Klare, M. T. (2012). *The Race for What's Left: The Global Scramble for the World's Last Resources.* New York, Metropolitan Books.

Lea, T. (2012). "When Looking for Anarchy, Look to the State: Fantasies of regulation in forcing disorder within the Australian Indigenous estate." *Critique of Anthropology* 32(2), 109-124.

Lea, T. (2014). *Darwin.* Sydney, NewSouth Books.

Lea, T. (2020). *Wild Policy* Stanford, Stanford University Press.

Lea, T. and S. Rollo (2016). "A Servant is Not Greater Than His Master: American Primacy in Australian Security." In *Hearts and Minds: US Cultural Management in 21st Century Foreign Relations*, edited by M. Chambers. Bern, Peter Lang. 17-42.

Lea, T., K. Howey and J. O'Brien. (2018). "Waging Paperfare: Subverting the Damage of Extractive Capitalism in Kakadu." *The Australian Journal of Anthropology* 18(3), 305-19.

Lockwood, D. (1966). *Australia's Pearl Harbour: Darwin, 1942.* Melbourne: Cassell Australia.

Michel, T. and A. Taylor (2012). "Death by a Thousand Grants? The Challenge of Grant Funding Reliance for Local Government Councils in the Northern Territory of Australia." *Local Government Studies* 38(4), 485-500.

Mignolo, W. D. (1992). "The Darker Side of the Renaissance: Colonization and the Discontinuity of the Classical Tradition." *Renaissance Quarterly* 45(4), 808-828.

Mosse, D. and D. Lewis. (2006). "Theoretical Approaches to Brokerage and Translation in Development." In *Development Brokers and Translators: The Ethnography of Aid and Agencies*, edited by D. Lewis and D. Mosse. Bloomfield CT, Kumarian Press. 1-26.

Nading, A. (2012). "Dengue Mosquitos Are Single Mothers: Biopolitics Meets Ecological Aesthetics in Nicaraguan Community Health Work." *Cultural Anthropology* 27(4), 572-596.

Neimanis, A. (2016). *Bodies of Water: Posthuman Feminist Phenomenology*. London, Bloomsbury (Kindle Edition).

Neu, D. (2000). "Accounting and Accountability Relations: Colonization, Genocide and Canada's First Nations." *Accounting, Auditing & Accountability Journal* 13(3), 268-288.

Nixon, R. (2011). *Slow Violence and the Environmentalism of the Poor*. Cambridge, MA. Harvard University Press.

Oliver, D. (1986). "Skin." *London Review of Books* 8(21), 14.

Pasternak, S. and T. Dafnos, (2017). "How Does a Settler State Secure the Circuitry of Capital?" *Environment and Planning D: Society and Space* 36(4), 739-757.

Povinelli, E. (2016). "Dear So and So of So, I Write Regarding Toxic Sovereignties in Windjarrameru." In *Public Servants: Art and the Crisis of the Common Good*, edited by J. Burton, S. Jackson and D. Willsdon. Cambridge MA, New Museum & MIT Press.

Povinelli, E. A. (2011). *Economies of Abandonment: Social Belonging and Endurance in Late Liberalism*. Durham, NC, Duke University Press.

Steffen, W., Hughes, L., Alexander, D., Rice, M., (2017). "Cranking Up the Intensity: Climate Change and Extreme Weather Events." https://www.climatecouncil.org.au/uploads/1b331044fb03fd0997c4a4946705606b.pdf, Climate Change Council of Australia.

Stokes, J. L. (1846). *Discoveries in Australia* (Volume 2); with an Account of the Coasts and Rivers Explored and Surveyed During the Voyage of H.M.S. Beagle in the Years 1837-38-39-40-41-42-43 by the Lords Commissioners of the Admiralty. Also A Narrative of Captain Owen Stanley's Visits to the Islands of the Arafura Sea. London, T. and W.Boone, 29 New Bond Street.

Terzon, Emilia. (2016). "How Darwin's iconic mangroves are fighting back against rising sea levels and climate change." *ABC Radio*, 3 May, retrieved from https://www.abc.net.au/news/2016-05-04/darwin-mangroves-battling-sea-level-rises/7379744

Viveiros de Castro, E. (2013). "The Relative Native." *HAU: Journal of Ethnographic Theory* 3(3), 473-502.

Vizener, G. (2009). *Native Liberty: Natural Reason and Cultural Survivance*. Lincoln and London, University of Nebraska Press.

Vizenor, G. (1994). *Manifest Manners: Narratives on Postindian Survivance*. Lincoln and London, University of Nebraska Press.

Wild, R. and P. Anderson. (2007). Ampe Akelyernemane Meke Mekarle "Little Children are Sacred": Report of the Northern Territory Board of Inquiry into the Protection of Aboriginal Children from Sexual Abuse. Darwin, Northern Territory Government.

Woinarski, J. C. Z., A. A. Burbidge, et al. (2015). "Ongoing unraveling of a continental fauna: Decline and extinction of Australian mammals since European settlement." *PNAS* 112(15), 4531-4540.

Zhao, Y., X. Zhang, et al. (2016). *Northern Territory burden of disease study: Fatal burden of disease and injury, 2004–2013*. Darwin, Northern Territory Department of Health.

Tess Lea

24 Skilling Up for the Anthropocene

Stephanie LeMenager

My approach to skill, as a theory of practice and the foundation for a more ecological and repair-oriented genre of humanism, begins with a book (John Stilgoe's *Shallow Water Dictionary*), progresses through a discussion of artist (Zina Saro-Wiwa), and ends with a series of novels (Butler). Detouring through plumbing, electrical repair, the culture of Preppers, and the archival salvage made central to the Environmental Digital Humanities, I have been deliberately capacious in my designation of what skill can be, and of the diverse skills that are needed for Anthropocene education. The pedagogies of the Environmental Humanities have always been practice-oriented, and in fact the field, still in formation, is called to practice by worldly needs. Skill as concept and practice offers one way to think about the futures of labor, of multispecies relationship, and of humanism—if we want it. At the same time, troubling the notion of "skill" (decoupling it from *metrics*) remains a central problem for education in a U.S. epoch of perhaps final, fatal assault on public services and goods.

The U.S. landscape historian John Stilgoe's 1990 volume *Shallow Water Dictionary* is, alongside Bill McKibben's *The Death of Nature* (1989), one of the earliest examples of climate change literature for a popular audience. Unlike McKibben's volume, Stilgoe's has not proven to *be* popular, although it still is possible to find a paperback edition of the dictionary in print. Like recent environmentalist print projects that offer "keywords" and "lexicons" for the era of the Sixth Extinction, *Shallow Water Dictionary* lays out a conceptual and linguistic guide to mitigate the shifting ground conditions of everyday life as climate change makes itself felt. It is an attempt at cultural mitigation of terror and grief. Stilgoe's revitalization of words that refer to defunct estuarine practices of life and work presumes no new worlds, just an homage to fading practice. The archaic terms of art for shallow water boating (terms like "guzzle" and "gundalow") that sluice through Stilgoe's essay in defense of our disappearing wetlands function to orient us within estuarine labors. The terms are Stilgoe's virtual "sea-marks," a word that he reminds us has meant "a point of land, or an object on land [...] to assist mariners" (14). Posing as both essayist and sailor, Stilgoe "pulls" his own sixteen-foot rowboat throughout the lyrical dictionary, using it to exemplify forgotten skills—the boat is named "Essay," after another skill we might conceive as forgotten. He describes his project of rowing/writing the Massachusetts wetlands as "a sort of salvage operation of words drifting from dictionary English [which] may serve to *moor* the terminology of estuary English" (11).

Stilgoe says that he intends to provoke topographical curiosity in the young, who have forgotten or never learned how to use maritime maps, and he attempts to preserve through his brief chronicle "a place [filled with life] facing extinction as the earth warms and the sea level rises" (11). He offers a dictionary of archaic speech as a bulwark to rising seas. Estuary English itself is diminishing just as estuaries themselves resolve into ocean, as adults fail to teach children the fundamentals of boating and sea harvesting. But in its increasing distance from regular practice the language also becomes, like poetry, unfamiliar and defamiliarizing, burnished, strange.

As I work my way circuitously toward the project of "skill," let's briefly revisit Stilgoe's description of his effort—which, again, marks one of the first efforts at climate change literary art. Again, Stilgoe calls it "a sort of salvage operation of words drifting from dictionary English [which] may serve to *moor* the terminology of estuary English" (11). *Moor*, meaning to fasten a drifting vessel with a cable, approaches another meaning of "moor" here, as fen or marsh. Stilgoe wants to hold fast the wetlands that are slipping away: that is the poetic conceit. As if what I elsewhere have called the geological mourning known as coastal subsidence could be halted by a raft of words (LeMenager 2014,102). This looks like a conservationist rendition of Romantic, linguistic primitivism, for instance Emerson's wish to "fasten" words to natural facts—in the essay *Nature*, or Thoreau's obsession with etymologizing language towards matter. "[My boat]

Stephanie LeMenager

Essay pokes and pulls...probing the utterly common landscape of the salt marshes," Stilgoe writes. "And always, always sounding the depths of common speech...vernacular alongshore speech fading from dictionary English" (43).

An elegiac project—but, I would argue, also a project that falls within what the literary historian Michael Ziser has named "the aesthetics of Transition," by which he meant the aesthetics associated with living in the Anthropocene and living through the chaotic end times of the energy regime of fossil fuels (181). In the inevitable loss of estuary English and the handcraft—rowing and sea harvesting—that it recounts, Stilgoe offers words—but not too many. His book is almost a proxy for the silence of the words no longer used, the skills slipping away. His quiet prose, speaking for extinct or near-extinct terms of art, holds within it both the silence of disuse (e.g. these fading lifeways) and the silence of practices that are bodily, focused on the empirical world. The relative quietness of Stilgoe's book offers to us a site not of academic debate or critique, but a site for reimagining the significance of language, and therefore humanism, in a time of profound ecological change. He notes that, "in the quiet, the old language barely whispers" (11). "The quiet" is the marsh as it is known by bodies in practice—the rower, rowing the boat, with the oar that Stilgoe describes as "an instrument, not a tool, something for <u>precise</u> work" (22). *Shallow Water Dictionary* marks the receding of language to the quiet embrace of co-constituting bodies (e.g. the intermingling of human and nature at work that Karl Marx, in his own poetic conceit for labor as an intimate exchange of bodily energies, calls "metabolism").[1] As a site where language hits its limits as an epistemological or ontological key, the dictionary humbles the Anthropocene idea insofar as that concept has been borne forward by rhetorics of human technological triumph or catastrophic extinction. We find the crisis of an existentially lonely humanism in the era of climate collapse to be not death per se, not apocalypse, but the silent rower, plying his instruments for precise work, work that respects the integrity of marsh and barnacle. Such practice engages the human while at the same time emphasizing our interdependence with non-humans, water, fish, and tools—our humility.

I begin with *Shallow Water Dictionary* because I spent a recent academic year in the Northeastern USA, walking among its wetlands, because I think it a beautiful and largely unknown book, and because I see it as a fine example of what I'll call vernacular post-humanism. My use of the term "vernacular post-humanism" is not intended to valorize post-humanism as a philosophical movement, if it were possible to do such a thing, given the diversity of thought that has been understood as posthumanist, from Donna Haraway's feminist science studies to Bruno Latour's Actor-Network-Theory to Stacy Alaimo's and Susan Hekman's material feminism to Jane Bennett's vitalist OOO to mel chen's gender-bending animism. This essay was written as an opportunity to engage with self-proclaimed posthumanists, who invited the essay, and my hope here is to bring what I understand as the varied posthumanisms down to earth by seeking the limits of the humanist project in the prosaic rhythms of work.

I think of skill as the site where human craft meets worldly force. As a concept, skill is profoundly humanist. Its etymological history, sunk in Old Norse and German ideas of *discernment*, attests to its close relationship to Reason, perhaps the ultimate fantasy of humanism from the eras of Enlightenment aspiration and colonialism. Still, I would suggest that the concept of skill has remained humble, assigned more often to so-called peasants than to elites, and it is largely about working with recalcitrant non-humans, and mastering—if anything—an intermediary and not/only/human language. All of these qualities—physicality, antithesis to language, wearing away at human force—make skilled work a practice that mocks at human transcendence, throwing the project of humanism off kilter. Skill has been with human populations arguably forever, now often most readily identified with rural or working-class or subsistence contexts than otherwise. It is sought after within academic culture as a means of self-justification as well as survival-oriented pedagogy in what is arguably the catastrophic end-times of neoliberal social economy.

Stephanie LeMenager

To think about skill is to think small, not in order to turn away from the vastness of the crises at hand but rather to re-ground oneself in first principles that may represent paths forward, from one day or even one hour to the next. The current academic debate launched by Alf Hornborg, an anthropologist and professor of Human Ecology, singles out "the environmental humanities" and in particular those posthumanists (Donna Haraway, Anna Tsing, and Jason Moore) whom Hornborg accuses of "dithering while the planet burns" (61). Hornborg's critique is ultimately about what constitutes disciplinary skill, or which disciplines can be said to practice skilled labor. He posits the work of social science as "to communicate clear and analytically rigorous arguments" (62) while the work of the humanities is to offer evocative "poetry" that sounds like tipsy dinner conversation (62). Hornborg also eschews emotionalism and memoir within scholarly prose, and he distrusts feminists who train dogs or forage mushrooms in contrast to men, like himself, who farm. Hornborg decries the inexplicable popularity of hazy thought, whose lack of rigor makes its practitioners, he claims, handmaidens to neoliberalism.

As a humanities scholar who bridles at Hornborg's narrow definition of "the environmental humanities" –let alone his misogyny, I nonetheless do appreciate what he recognizes as posthumanist nostalgia for the multispecies worlds of farming, for instance, that suburban and urban academics rarely know, of the "urge to verbalize a mode of experiencing the world that lies just beyond their reach, but remains fundamental to a great many people on the planet" (66). This yearning outward toward environed work, toward a life embedded in skilled cooperation with non-humans, is not only a characteristic of academics (let alone humanities scholars). We can see comparable projects toward what I'll call *a new materialism of practice* in popular movements as diverse as prepping, the "scrapping" and refurbishing of Rust Belt U.S. cities, and even the disciplined training of the anti-fascist militias known as Antifa. Of course White Nationalist militias also can be said to be "skilling"—I do not intend the term "skill" to be purely positive or politically progressive. It extends into gun usage across many groups. My point is that as the U.S. state fails or willfully destroys itself, and as the global economy becomes increasingly volatile, a significant set of countercultural actors are skilling up for the Anthropocene. To the extent that the Environmental Humanities talks about foraging and crocheting and all manner of DIY, it participates in this cultural rising tide. It also participates by expanding the skill set of humanities practitioners—into public writing, documentary filmmaking, ethnography, and increasing collaboration across disciplinary boundaries.

I began to think about skill as a way to understand posthumanism as related to the current hunger for practice, in both academic and North American popular cultures, in my encounter with the British-Nigerian artist Zina Saro-Wiwa's work on the Indigenous knowledge practices of the Ogoni people. This need to "skill up" that I identify as a response to Anthropocene disorder suggests a settler culture's anxieties about the neoliberal privatization of life, about the devaluing of work within a global service economy and the growing corporate assault upon all sovereignties, even those of settlers. I should emphasize here that I realize that Indigenous Traditional Ecological Knowledges (TEKs) do not exist for me, as a settler/trespasser. TEKs are not intended for my future, and what I learn from them may contribute more to what Eve Tuck and K. Wayne Yang identify as "white harm reduction" than to the incommensurable project of decolonization (Tuck and Wayne Yang 2012, 21). That said, white harm reduction is important to me. I will attempt to learn how to bring it about from whoever is generous enough to offer me a glimpse into their work. Saro-Wiwa was one such teacher. Briefly I acted as a consultant for her first solo exhibit at the Blaffer Gallery in Houston, titled *"Did You Know We Taught Them How to Dance?"* The exhibit highlighted the many skills of the Ogoni of the Niger Delta, where part of Saro-Wiwa's family resides. These skills include farming, fishing, traditional dancing, the carving of masks, and the almost balletic skill of eating with one's hands, which was denigrated as barbaric by the British. These Ogoni skills represented for Saro-Wiwa "what Oil can't understand," forms of practice and survival under the radar of Big Oil and the transnational power it represents. "What Oil can't understand" may also be unknowable to Northern environmentalists like myself, whom Saro-Wiwa places at closer proximity to Big Oil than I'd care to acknowledge, though acknowledge it I do (LeMenager 2016, 43).[2] As noted, these TEKs and their performance are not *for* me—but, still, they taught me something about cultural practice that flies under the radar of politics per se, and that makes it possible to live through, and stick with, political conflict and resistance. Saro-Wiwa also taught me that everyday skill could open ways of thinking what Sylvia Wynter has called alternative "genres of humanism" (Wynter and Scott 2000, 195-7). Here I imagine a humanism based in embedded practice, the work humans have so long done with non-human others.

I might also recast this way of thinking of skill as a vernacular post-humanism, in relation to my last project, the book *Living Oil*. *Living Oil* offers a literary and cultural history of what I call petro-modernity, by which I mean twentieth-century American modernity as it came about through the varied media of petroleum, from asphalt to film stock. Skill, as embodied, intra-active, knowledge-practice, can be recognized as an antidote to the disappearing of labor in the spectacular concept of modern energy, not to mention the automation made possible by that energy. Energy—as I learned in the writing of *Living Oil*—has been a charismatic concept that obscures both labor and power (LeMenager 2014, 4). I frequently return to the historian Richard White's materialist definition of power as the ability to command the energy, and labor, of others (7). White places his understanding of energy within colonialist domination, as he writes about how the so-called voyage of discovery of the Lewis and Clark expedition used Indigenous, Métis and lower-status French Canadians to carry their canoes and baggage during portage. The colonialist command of energy to secure power can be traced from such simple acts of using economically marginal, racialized bodies to the more spectacular and less transparent "bioderegulation" of labor in wealthier-world economies, which Teresa Brennan recounted in her fine book of the early 2000s, *Globalization and*

Its Terrors (19). (Consider the sleep deprivation recounted in Barbara Ehrenreich's now classic *Nickel and Dimed* as one specific example of how working bodies in the U.S. service economy cannot live by prior, hard-won regulations—such as the eight-hour day). Because of the obscuring of labor and the fundamental metabolic exchange it implies in the age of neoliberalism (Marx cites the "metabolic rift" coming much earlier, in the era of industrial capitalism) skill also lies at the center of varied energy Transition social movements and projects. Skill figures as a way out of petro-capitalism, sometimes a way *back*—reminiscent of North American back-to-the-land movements of the 1960s. But, with more urgency and fear.

The novelist and essayist Amitav Ghosh argued in his recent book *The Great Derangement* that traditional knowledges and skills might be the only safeguard for the world's poor as climate change and its political consequences come to ground.[3] Some settlers in the wealthier world also remember and cultivate skills, which may be helpful in if not remaking the world then in cobbling pieces of it back together into something more broken but, we can hope, more just. Getting in touch with settler relationships to place, often not far distant from academics of my generation—how many of us, I learn, have had farmers as grandparents—should not be done as a "move to innocence" to erase the fact of the Indigenous communities whose land our ancestors took for themselves either knowingly or blindly, forcibly or passively.[4] We must not forget these settler ancestors, their violence from which we profit as well as their relationship to animals and plants whose lives they tended for profit and for love. Ancestors whose abilities to survive predate the making of the Progressive state in the U.S. starting in the early twentieth century might help us in some quite specific ways to live with a failed and increasingly violent state. It also is useful to remember that the racist violence of the current administration in the U.S. is a reiteration of the frontier ideology that justified the (failed) genocide of Indigenous Americans.

The literatures and arts of the Transition Movement—a movement both inciting energy transition and responding to the

Stephanie LeMenager

threat of scarcities of energy, food, and water—have been focused upon what the artist Brett Bloom calls the "breakdown" of modern subjectivities and transition into what we might call Anthropocene ones—many of which have been associated with craft skills and cultures of repair. In summer camp-like workshops called "break down/break downs," Bloom trains participants to disassemble their "petro-subjectivity."[5] Similar ideas are present in peak oil literatures and handbooks by Rob Hopkins, James Howard Kunstler, and others. To paraphrase Matthew Schneider Mayerson's excellent sociological account of the peak oil movement, *Peak Oil: Apocalyptic Environmentalism and Libertarian Political Culture*, the U.S. Transition movement of the early aughts espoused Libertarian notions of absolute autonomy, disaggregated from political activism for the sake of rebuilding an effective democratic state. "Skilling Up for the Anthropocene" can be synonymous with a wide range of political and cultural affiliations, from Libertarian prepping to hipster hobbyism to anti-racist Transition movements to urban community-aid groups like those that sprang up in the wake of Hurricane Sandy, in response to the failures of FEMA.[6] Such affiliations and cultural identities develop and morph, and they are riven by internal differences.

Again, "skilling up" does not have a singular political flavor. Preppers live on a broad political spectrum across conservative, evangelical, Latter Day Saints (Mormon), and progressive or left-Libertarianism. Their fear of state failure—particularly in light of a catastrophic "event" like nuclear war or a weather freak—is not unfounded, even if their patriarchal survivalism alarms me. "Remember what I said long ago about learning new tips, tricks, and adapting being the keys to survival?," one well-known prepper bloggist writes, as he recounts his surprise at finding in the LDS church—which he did not consider an ally—an excellent source of canned foods for emergency storage. This *bricoleur* mentality is to some extent repeated in the varied dictionaries and lexicons intended by academics and artists to culturally prepare us for Anthropocene living, energy transition, resistance and adaptation to climate change. For example, Bloom's previously cited "Break Down Break Down" website, with its list of significant terms like "Petro-Subjectivity." Or the scholar Karen Pinkus' *Fuel: A Speculative Dictionary*, an ingenious attempt "to open up potential ways of interacting with substances (real and imaginary), by wrenching them out of narrative (violently in some cases), and placing them in the form of an idiosyncratic dictionary so that they could eventually be replaced by users into new narratives" (128).

Because of my own belief in a robust idea of public(s) (capacious and plural) and the necessity for cultivating public goods, I am interested in building self-aware cultures of practice and allowing skill as a concept to converse with "higher" theories and cultures of the Anthropocene, such as post-humanist philosophies. How to build an ethical and intellectual culture around the everyday more pressing necessities of repair—as houses in the U.S. Northeast flood due to record deep freeze, as mudslides destroy entire communities and road networks in southern California—will be a primary challenge for education in the Anthropocene. It is not too early for the Environmental Humanities to consider how vocational education in the so-called trades and culture-making complement one another. The witty Climate Fiction of the British author Saki Lloyd, who writes for young adults, emphasizes the desirability (and even sexiness) of would-be plumbers and electricians among Anthropocene teenagers in the UK. Lloyd also emphasizes the biocultural importance of making music, poetry, visual art, and novels. In the academy, digital Humanities scholars following Bethany Novwiskie have made strong arguments for the necessity of reimagining their work in terms of projects of repair and salvage. If skill fails to readily fit posthumanist thought, even as its vernacular cousin, perhaps it lays the practical or practice-oriented foundation for a new genre of humanism. This genre of humanism-at-work concerns itself with repair and maintenance rather than the endless growth associated with human species potential under capitalism.

In conclusion, I want to speak briefly of the novel as a performance of a particular kind of skill, an engagement between

Stephanie LeMenager

human intelligence and world, and more specifically of the Cli Fi novel as potentially an appropriate technology for the Anthropocene and a site of Skilling Up. This coda draws from my work with Jesse Oak Taylor and Tobias Meneley, in their collection *Anthropocene Reading,* where I discuss climate fiction within a larger treatment of the novel as a genre of the "everyday," a form of art that has registered habitual experience and the ordinariness of work as background conditions for the humanist enterprise—think of Hemingway's precise evocations of flipping a pancake, Jennifer Egan's account of underwater ship construction in her recent, magnificent *Manhattan Beach* (2017, 221). Although I would generally concur with Nicholas Carr's depiction of the novel as a training ground for a now obsolescent form of human intelligence, I also haven't failed to notice that some novels, and merely the act of reading, are featured in the varied Anthropocene cultures of skill, craft, and repair (123). I recently encountered a thirty-something man on a flight to Portland who explained to me that reading a novel is like listening to vinyl—textured, grounding. Analog intelligence to counter digital malaise? This Millennial sociology of reading merits further investigation.

Take as a case in point Octavia Butler's *Parable* novel series, and the surge of what I call "Butlermania" that has accompanied the intensification of Anthropocene demagoguery and Anthropocene weather, from roughly the aftermath of Hurricane Katrina to the election of U.S. president Donald Trump. The outpouring of countercultural fan fiction, performance, and activism in response to Butler's *Parable* novels attests that she offers compelling strategies for shaping pockets of anti-racist, sustainable community. Early in *Parable of the Sower* (1993), the novel's teenaged heroine, Lauren Olamina, offers her best friend Joanne a lesson in how to live on, into a world of unprecedented "tornadoes…blizzard…epidemic" that will be governed in the U.S. by a white nationalist president intent on "setting the country back a hundred years," a violent political project announced by the slogan "Make America Great Again." (The latter a coincidence with Trump's "MAGA" slogan that has earned Butler credit for prophecy). Lauren's lesson suggests a process of self-education that we might call skilling up. The topic of how to educate oneself for survival, including cultural survival, is introduced in Butler's novel as a conversation between the two young women.

> "....We're fifteen! What can we do?"
>
> "We can get ready. That's what we've got to do now. Get ready for what's going to happen, get ready to survive it, get ready to make a life afterward. Get focused on arranging to survive so that we can do more than just get batted around by crazy people, desperate people, thugs, and leaders who don't know what they're doing!" (55)

The fact that two fifteen year olds hold this momentous discussion puts *Parable of the Sower* in line with several YA Anthropocene novels that recognize the question of the future as one which both affects young people most consequentially and in essence turns adults into virtual adolescents, given how unprepared many of us are for climate change and its collateral damages. *Parable of the Sower* intends to help the reader grow up into a realization of the need for socio-ecological change, beginning with a new kind of education which involves both studying up on local botany and cultivating seemingly less pragmatic gifts, like hyper-empathy.

Not surprisingly, the infectious repetition of Lauren's "get ready" features in one version of Bernice Johnson Reagon's and Toshi Reagon's operatic adaptation of *Parable of the Sower,* a Civil Rights-era inspired, committed musical performance which may do for Butler's novel what theater adaptation did for *Uncle Tom's Cabin*—eg. make it the centerpiece of a movement, in this case an anti-racist, climate justice movement.[7] In *Parable of the Sower,* skilling up includes future-envisioning and attaining education, especially literacy—which some readers have noted is foregrounded here as a means of survival as much as it was in the nineteenth-century slave narratives that Butler touches upon throughout her extensive *oeuvre.*[8] In a chilling response to an audience member's queries about survival at a performance

Stephanie LeMenager

of the Reagons' operatic *Parable* in Abu Dhabi, Toshi Reagon noted that history is full of stories of peoples who failed to survive, living in extreme vulnerability and asking themselves for too long if it is time to change. Audience members elaborated upon the idea of the theater as a space of refuge in our time of extensive habitat loss, from which transformative change might be launched.[9]

The varied skills of culture-making—including the making of narrative, history, philosophy, the visual arts, performance, and song—are foundational to systemic transition. Skilling up demands a fundamental reassessment of the meanings and force of all kinds of work, including the labors of the arts and humanities.

Notes

1   See John Bellamy Foster's ingenious reading of Marxian metabolism (2000). A particularly succinct reading of the term—and citation from Marx's *Capital,* Vol. 1, appears on p. 157.

2   Kyle Powys Whyte writes compellingly about the importance of recognizing TEKs as about Indigenous governance and futurities (as opposed to settler futurities) in "What Do Indigenous Knowledges Do for Indigenous Peoples?" (forthcoming) and elsewhere. Settler/trespasser cultures are increasingly interested in Indigenous philosophy and science as we see ourselves experiencing what seems the end-times of settler modernities.

3   Ghosh writes of traditional knowledges and skills, "The cumulative effect [of the Great Acceleration] is the extinction of exactly those forms of traditional knowledge, material skills, art, and ties to community that might provide succor to vast numbers of people around the world—and especially to those who are still bound to the land—as the impacts intensify. The very speed with which the crisis is now unfolding may be the one factor that will preserve some of these resources" (161).

4   Tuck and Yang discuss varied settler/trespasser "moves to innocence," essentially our denials of complicity or profit from our ancestors' colonialist projects (10)

5   For an Introduction to Bloom's varied projects on petro-subjectivity, see https://www.breakdownbreakdown.net/petro-subjectivity/. Accessed June 20, 2018.

6   Ashley Dawson does an excellent job of describing such community-aid groups in NYC in the wake of Sandy. I'm thinking particularly of Dawson's chapter "Disaster Communism," 233-273.

7   For more on this terrific new opera, see: https://www.para-bleopera.com/.

8   For discussion of the *Parable* novels as neo-slave narrative or commentary on slave narrative (see Madhu Dubey 345-363; Sylvia Mayer; Joo 279-299). An extensive catalog of readings on this topic can be found in the MLA bibliography database. Shelly Streeby's *Imagining the Future of Climate Change*, not yet published at the time of writing, offers an excellent discussion of Butler as a prophet of climate justice.

9   Remembrance of audience conversation with Toshi Reagon following the performance of the Reagons' *Parable of the Sower*, opera, at NYU Abu Dhabi Arts Center. November 9, 2017.

Works Cited

Bellamy Foster, John. (2000). *Marx's Ecology: Materialism and Nature*. New York: Monthly Review Press, .

Bloom, Brett. (2015). "Petro-Subjectivity." BreakdownBreakdown. BkdnBkdn Press. Retrieved from https://breakdownbreakdown.net/petro-subjectivity/.

Brennan, Teresa. (2003). *Globalization and Its Terrors: Daily Life in the West*. New York: Routledge.

Carr, Nicholas. (2011). *The Shallows: What the Internet Is Doing to Our Brains*. New York: W.W. Norton and Company.

Dawson, Ashley. (2017). *Extreme Cities: The Perils and Promise of Urban Life in the Age of Climate Change*. New York: Verso.

Dubey, Madhu. (2013). "Octavia Butler's Narratives of Enslavement." *Novel: A Forum on Fiction* 46(3), 345-363.

Ghosh, Amitav. (2016). *The Great Derangement: Climate Change and the Unthinkable*. Chicago: U. Chicago.

Hornborg, Alf. (2017). "Dithering While the Planet Burns: Anthropologists' Approaches to the Anthropocene." *Reviews in Anthropology* 46(2-3), 61-77.

Joo, Hee-Jung Serenity. (2011). "Old and New Slavery, Old and New Racisms: Strategies of Science Fiction in Octavia Butler's Parables Series." *Extrapolation* 52(3), 279-299.

LeMenager, Stephanie. (2017). "Climate Change and the Struggle for Genre." In Tobias Menely and Jesse Oak Taylor, eds. *Anthropocene Reading: Literary History in Geologic Times*. University Park: Penn State.

LeMenager, Stephanie. (2016). "Eden if We Dare." In *Zina Saro-Wiwa: Did You Know We Taught Them How to Dance?*, ed. Amy L. Powell. Houston: Blaffer Art Museum and Krannert Art Museum.

LeMenager, Stephanie. (2014). *Living Oil: Petroleum Culture in the American Century*. New York: Oxford.

Lloyd, Saci. (2008). *The Carbon Diaries 2015*. New York: Holiday House.

Lloyd, Saci. (2010). *The Carbon Diaries 2017. New York: Holiday House.*

Mayer, Sylvia. (2003). "Genre and Environmentalism: Octavia Butler's Parable of the Sower, Speculative Fiction, and African American Slave Narrative." In *Restoring the Connection to the Natural World: Essays on the African American Environmental Imagination*, ed. Sylvia Mayer. New York: Transaction Publishers. 175-196.

Nowviskie, Bethany. (2014). "Digital Humanities in the Anthropocene." 10 July. Bethany Nowviskie. WordPress. https://www.nowviskie.org

Parable Staff. (2015-2019). "Octavia E. Butler's Parable of the Sower, an Opera by Toshi Reagon and Bernice Johnson Reagon." *ParableOpera*. https://www.parableopera.com/.

Pinkus, Karen. (2016). *Fuel: A Speculative Dictionary*. Minneapolis: U. Minnesota. Kindle Edition.

Tuck, Eve and K. Wayne Yang. (2012). "Decolonization Is Not a Metaphor." *Decolonization: Indigeneity, Education, and Society* 1(1), 1-40.

Schneider-Mayerson, Matthew. (2015). *Peak Oil: Apocalyptic Environmentalism and Libertarian Political Culture*. Chicago: U. Chicago P.

Stilgoe, John. (2003). *Shallow Water Dictionary*. Princeton: Princeton Architectural Press.

Streeby, Shelley. (2018). *Imagining the Future of Climate Change: World-Making through Science Fiction and Activism.* Berkeley: UC Press.

White, Richard. (1995). *The Organic Machine: The Remaking of the Columbia River.* New York: Hill and Wang.

Wynter, Sylvia and David Scott. (2000). "The Re-Enchantment of Humanism: An Interview with Sylvia Wynter." *Small Axe: A Caribbean Journal of Criticism* 4 (September) 119-207.

Ziser, Michael G. (2011). "Home Again: Peak Oil, Climate Change, and the Aesthetics of Transition." In *Environmental Criticism for the Twenty-First Century*, eds. Stephanie LeMenager, Teresa Shewry, Ken Hiltner. London and New York: Routledge. 81-195.

25 Reflections on a Survival Skills Workshop: A Response to Stephanie LeMenager by Jennifer Hamilton with Endnotes by Tessa Zettel (presenter) and Kate Judith (participant)

Jennifer Hamilton

I organised "Weathering the Apocalypse: a Survival Skills Workshop" as part of the event series "Feminist, Queer, Anticolonial Propositions for Hacking the Anthropocene II: Weathering". It was at the headquarters of the River Canoe Club of NSW in Tempe, NSW in May 2017. The idea was to practically model an alternative vision of what counts as a skill to survive in a warming world, and also to reclaim the concept of survival from the militarized and high-anxiety "prepper" culture (the bunker, the freezedried food, ammunition stockpiles, the apolcalyptic vision). Instead, we wanted to consider survival outside the context of the emergency, in a time of slow violence (Nixon, 2011). Or, indeed, survival as a type of "weathering" (Neimanis and Hamilton, 2018): a banal, durational and differentiated experience guided by a range of ecosocial forces mostly beyond the control of an individual. But also, given the demographic of the day—a cohort of predominantly white, university-educated individuals—it was important to note that many of us had never had to really struggle to survive. For many less privileged in the world, the concept of survival is not a novel theory to speculate on over cups of tea. And so, in this regard our group was perhaps more like the preppers than we'd like to believe; we were a group with the luxury, time, resources, shelter and food to reflect on how we might want to practice survival. Unlike the preppers though, the survival skills we explored during the day were more community oriented, creative, speculative and hopeful. In this regard, we might think about the skill workshop in relation to Gerald Vizenor's concept of "survivance" (2008)—a name for the creativity indigenous peoples use to persist and live in settler-colonialism, beyond the basics of survival. We did not co-opt this term as a name for our activities, but the workshop was specifically inviting more privileged to consider a less anxious, less defensive, less self-protective model of survival, one that can be understood as creative and one that, in time, may be able to express solidarity with other ecosocial struggles and skill-share with others, instead of defending the nest until the death for our kind alone.

• • •

After kayaking down the Wolli Creek and Cooks River—a tidal estuary to the south of Sydney—I overheard a comment about the varying degrees of skill displayed by the participants. While some seemed comfortable hopping into the canoe, others nearly fell in the cold and dirty water, unable to balance on such a vessel. In the context of thinking about skill, this particular activity revealed a diversity of levels. Kayaking was evidently not a skill everyone needed to survive in Sydney in 2017. And indeed, the activity was not designed to suggest kayaking should be an essential skill, but rather as a question and a prompt for creative speculation or "design thinking": what might transport look like in a time of climate change?

Climate change mitigation is often conceptualized as a technological problem, where human skill-sets are fixed and instead the technologies need adaptation. The electric car is the most obvious example here. Driving is the necessary and time-less skill. Therefore, greening the car, rather than changing the skill, is the obvious solution; enter Elon Musk, venture capital-ists and the inexplicable hype around electric cars and, as we from British colonies say, "bob's your uncle!". In this context, the transport infrastructures of the fossil fuel age remain, the skills of the driver remain, but the vehicle is replaced. But is it really possible to compartmentalise transition and mitigation in this way? Some would like to think so, perhaps because the question of what comes next is difficult, political and speculative (rather than straightforward and profitable). The question is not only what technology do we use to get around, but for what purposes

Jennifer Hamilton

are we moving? Driving from the suburbs to the city is to serve capital. Perhaps the speculative vehicles of a climate-changed world are of wholly different conceptual order, where the "driver" whistles and dances rather than sits, changes gears and steers. And where the work engaged at the destination serves a radically different political ecology.

In 2015 I published "Labour" for the "Living Lexicon for the Environmental Humanities". This lexicon is, as Stephanie says in her essay, a "linguistic toolkit to mitigate the shifting ground conditions of everyday life as climate change makes itself felt" (LeMenager 2021). The problem with my argument in "labour" is that it suggests mitigation will need to be much more than rhetorical. It must be an embodied, radical re-skilling of the global workforce. I remember a colleague saying to me at the time something like: "I read your labour piece; it's great, but I had no idea you were a hardcore Marxist". But I'm not really. I've read some Marx, but not all three volumes of Capital. And this piece, the first thing I published after my PhD on the storm in *King Lear*, is wildly out of step of my other scholarship. But at that point I just wanted to get my hands dirty. Either I was going to become an activist and a market gardener, or an academic. But surely in this time one needs to be all three? This is because, as I argued then and stand by still now, "this situation was built, not conjured. Imagining the crisis as collectively wrought invokes the sweaty, material and embodied effort invested in making the crisis and invites speculation as to what kinds of labours it will take to actively create a different future." Trouble is, how to get there? What labours do we need to practice? What skills do we need to forget and what ones do we need to cultivate? And, of course, who is the "we", whose skills are more valuable to this radical world-changing project (perhaps not the skills that are most valuable in today's wage-labour hierarchy?)?

While many are working on this question in a mainstream context (more training pathways for people in renewable energy or organic farming), I think it is important to bring the more radical, if often theoretical, insights of cultural and literary studies to bear on thinking these questions too. This is in line with

Stephanie's interest in "building more self-conscious cultures of practice and allowing skill as a concept to converse with 'higher' theories of the Anthropocene, such as post-humanism" (LeMenager 2021). As a question, then, we ask: what skills are required to materially produce the kind of world we often seek in theory? [1] This was the question of the workshop too.

The design of this workshop the skills shared held both symbolic and practical weight. Participants were encouraged not to think about particular skills, like kayaking, as the true and essential skill decided by me as the pathway to proper survival, but rather to think about each skill in terms of genre, teleology and the potential political ecology it produces. The five skills were as follows:

1. Chicken Slaughter (FOOD): Genevieve Derwent

2. Darning (REPAIR): Tessa Zettel [2]

3. Kayaking (TRANSPORT): The Canoe Club: Kayaking

4. Siren Building (MUSIC/IRONY/ART): Pia van Gelder

5. Meditation (EMBODIMENT): Jennifer Hamilton

Each leader talked us through their particular experience with the skill and, where relevant, we engaged in the activity. We didn't all slaughter chickens, but we watched a film of this process and discussed the ethics of food production, sale and consumption. We were, however, able to darn our trousers, kayak down the creek, make a little siren-instrument and sit for 15 minutes inside our bodies in the late afternoon sun. What follows now are some notes I took on the day…

Notes

Gen Derwent: Runs a chicken farm outside Bega with her wife.

- Self-sustaining / Self-reliance is too much burden on the body. Skills must be shared. Community is key.

- Their project is a practical engagement with the question of how to think differently about the problem of the city and food?
- Industrial agriculture has a different TASTE and it doesn't taste very nice.

Tessa: An artist making time

- For Susie's mum "nothing is too damaged"; nothing is beyond repair
- Wild Darning is an embodied and intuitive skill
- The body has to learn with the object, the body becomes with the item being repaired
- YouTube is a repository of skills.

Pia: An artist that builds instruments

- Bread-board siren makings are "non-proprietorial circuits"
- It is almost like weaving with metal
- Sirens are "deceitful beings, instruments for obedience and warning". How can we hack this logic?
- By way of circuits; circuits are mechanisms for operationalizing energy for a particular purpose (not necessarily for deceit or warning).

Jennifer:

- I lead this skill. The idea was based on my own experience of cancer and the need to return to the body, despite wanting to escape it.
- I don't think it is straightforward to practice the self as mortal, but I do think that living on and with the planet requires openness to the terminal aspect of individual earthly life (even as we might seek a healthy, long life at the same time).

Figure 1. The Survival Skills Workshop at the Cooks River Canoe Club Headquarters. Photo by Jennifer Hamilton.

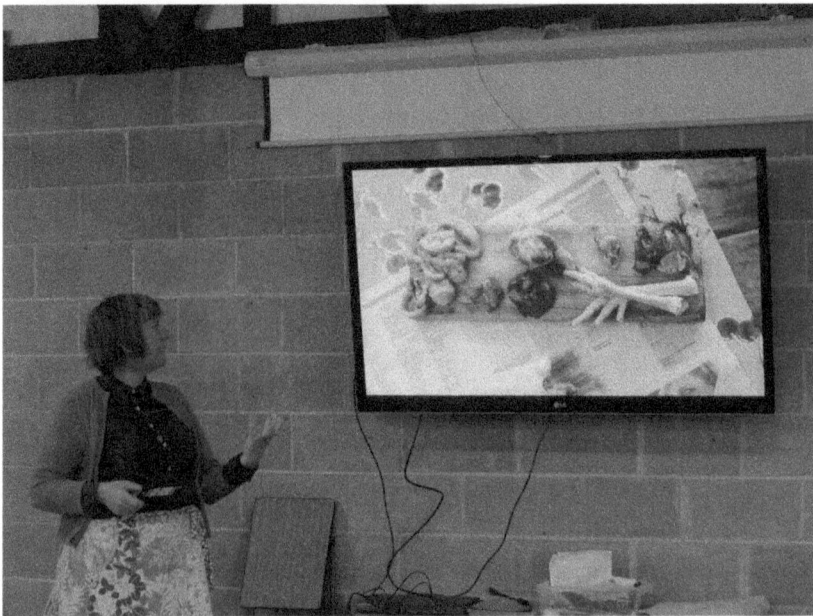

Figure 2. Genevieve Derwent from Autumn Farm in Bega talking about her small abatoir. Photo by Jennifer Hamilton.

Jennifer Hamilton

Figure 3. The group getting ready to canoe on the Cooks River. Photo by Jennifer Hamilton.

Figure 4. Laura McLauchlan and Karin Bolender getting ready to canoe. Photo by Jennifer Hamilton.

Figure 5. Astrida Neimanis and Susanne Pratt getting ready to canoe. Photo by Jennifer Hamilton.

Figure 6. Stephanie LeMenager leading a conversation about love. Photo by Jennifer Hamilton.

Figure 7. Tessa Zettel leading a workshop on bookmaking and darning. Photo by Jennifer Hamilton.

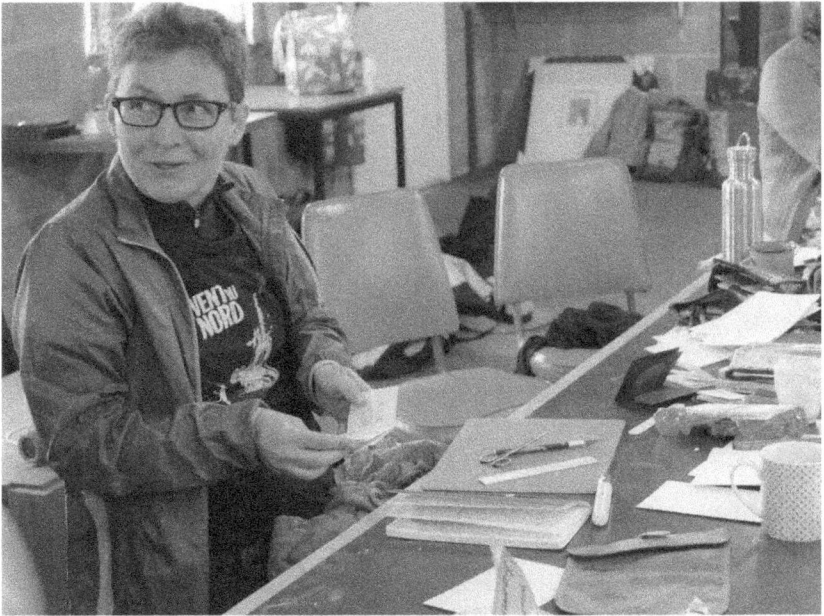

Figure 8. Stephanie LeMenager reading a small book. Photo by Jennifer Hamilton.

Figure 9. Pia van Gelder leading a siren making workshop. Photo by Jennifer Hamilton.

Figure 10. Pia van Gelder leading a siren making workshop. Photo by Jennifer Hamilton.

Jennifer Hamilton

Figure 11. Siren song. Photo by Jennifer Hamilton.

Figure 12. Basking in the afternoon sunshade. Photo by Jennifer Hamilton.

How do you know you have a skill?

- You do it with grace
- You are not afraid
- You have received recognition via invitations to demonstrate or employment
- You have affective comfort/stability when doing it
- Something emerges when you do it, rather than a mess
- Other people want to learn from you
- You can do it with attentiveness, a kind of effortless effort

At the end of the day we asked participants to offer one word that summarises skills for an alter-anthropocene:

Love – Laura M

Love – Stephanie

Wonder – Julie

Resistance – Karin

Vulnerability – Michael

Connection – Susie

Atrophy – Clare

Tardigrades – Josh

Potentiometer/Fraught – Astrida

Affinity – Laura X

Finitude – Denis

Reevaluation/Recalibration – Kate

Listening – Pia

Scale – Ali

Value – Tessa

Duration – Jen

Notes

1   by Kate Judith:

In rethinking skills for the Anthropocene we also need to acknowledge the innumerable new and altered skills that non-humans are inventing, practicing, and passing on to their kin and companions. As we canoed and discussed our human skills, we noticed the cormorant dexterously diving with well-practiced poise along the embankment and the mangrove leaves cleverly figuring their chemistry and osmotic differentials to tinker with the particular mix of salt, hydrocarbons, heavy metals and water the river mud provided for them that day. The crabs kept constant watch and practiced their rapid plunging moves into their holes whenever one of us moved closer to the mud bank. For many non-humans life in the Anthropocene has demanded changes in practice. That might mean changes in communication (as with many urban birds), migration routes, territorial range, or diet and food preparation. In turn, the Anthropocene calls us to develop and practice better skills for noticing, admiring and making space for the skills of non-humans.

2   by Tessa Zettel:

I can't recall exactly how I came to be leading a workshop on darning. Certainly, repairing holes in fabric is not something I have special expertise in, though I have watched my mother darn (for me) competently many a time. It transpired perhaps via murmurings of a darning circle in the works, *Gosh darn it!*, to which participants bring either mending skills or a contribution to a shared meal. Skills exchanged would then feed into a 'guide-to-darning' zine via the micropublishing platform Cloudship Press. In the lead-up to the workshop, between sewing piles of handmade books (also for the first time), I thus found myself scouring the internet and people around me for basic instructions and exemplary darns. As a seasoned interdisciplinary amateur, I'm not unaccustomed to picking up fragments of existing knowledge practices and seeing what they might become in the hands of a gathering. To this one I brought a tea towel darned immaculately by a great aunt in Germany at the turn of the century and from a friend's mother, a few remarkable pieces of 'wild darning' bordering on embroidery. Of course, the group itself had enough shared know-how to make a respectable go of the tears, moth-bites and holes otherwise spelling an early demise for those items selected for repair. And so, we threaded and wove our way through a practice of care that may be/have been commonplace to bodies enjoying a more lasting relationship with the objects around them.

Works Cited

Hamilton, Jennifer. (2015). "Labour" *Environmental Humanities* 6(1), 183–186.

LeMenager, Stephanie. (2021). "Skilling Up for the Anthropocene", in Hamilton, J., S. Reid, P. van Gelder, A. Neimanis, *Feminist Queer and Anticolonial Propositions for Hacking the Anthropocene: ARCHIVE.* London: Open Humanities Press.

Neimanis, Astrida and Jennifer Hamilton. (2018). "Weathering." *feminist review* 118, 80–84.

Nixon, Rob. (2011). *Slow Violence and the Environmentalism of the Poor.* Cambridge: Harvard University Press.

Vizenor, Gerald. (2008). "Aesthetics of Survivance: Literary Theory and Practice" in *Survivance: Narratives of Native Presence* Lincoln: University of Nebraska Press.

Part 3: Hacking the Anthropocene 3: Want (2018)

26 An Incantation for Love & Anger

Betty Grumble & Emma Maye Gibson

So there are these men /

and these men want power /

and to get that power they sell something they can't own /

they make up control /

they invent illusion /

and they don't realise /

baby /

they commit self harm /

they're killing themselves /

men are killing themselves /

men are killing themselves /

men are killing themselves /

they are killing us /

ooop baby!

but not ALL men /

not ALL men /

not ALL men /

wrapping the umbilical cord round their greedy gullets /

they are tying it in knots /

they are cracking like whip /

because that natural world they wanna price check /

stocktake /

they don't realise thats them /

thats us /

one dollar bid now one now one now /

two dollar bid now two now two now /

three, four SOLD to the man in the back /

ooh baby how much?

ooh baby how much?

LIFE can you take?

but life baby, Gaia /

she'll keep on going /

she'll bubble up and spit us out like a wound healing /

she'll bubble up and spit us out and she will keep on going /

but here we are /

gather together /

wanna feel something 'cause i'm a /

SEX CLOWN SEX CLOWN

and ooh yeah i've got big tits /

and ooh yeah i've got succulent bits /

and I am so, ready, to, GROW /

'cause we're like the soil /

we're gunna return to it /

we are water and air /

we are turning in it /

and i've got these petals /

and stems /

and a fresh new buzz /

and oh man you secrete /

I eat /

you secrete I eat /

I am so ready to fuck and be fucked /

I am so ready to move and be moved /

oh baby I am SO ready to grow /

i've got these canyons and precipice /

vine like sensibility /

reaching forward /

wrapping round /

I got a scent like rain first hitting /

I got stink like old wet world /

I breathe her /

I let her go /

and then /

I BLEED /

I slip my fingers inside /

women body / faggot body / different body /

gets stronger / resilient /

harden's up like those hard on's begging to be cut /

oh i've just had an idea /

i'm gunna end world hunger /

i'm gunna make a stew outta THIS CASTRATION FANTASY /

this environment /

this environment /

this environment, baby /

I wanna give birth /

Betty Grumble & Emma Maye Gibson

I wanna give birth /

I wanna give birth to your babies /

and their big green eyes will look up and me and say /

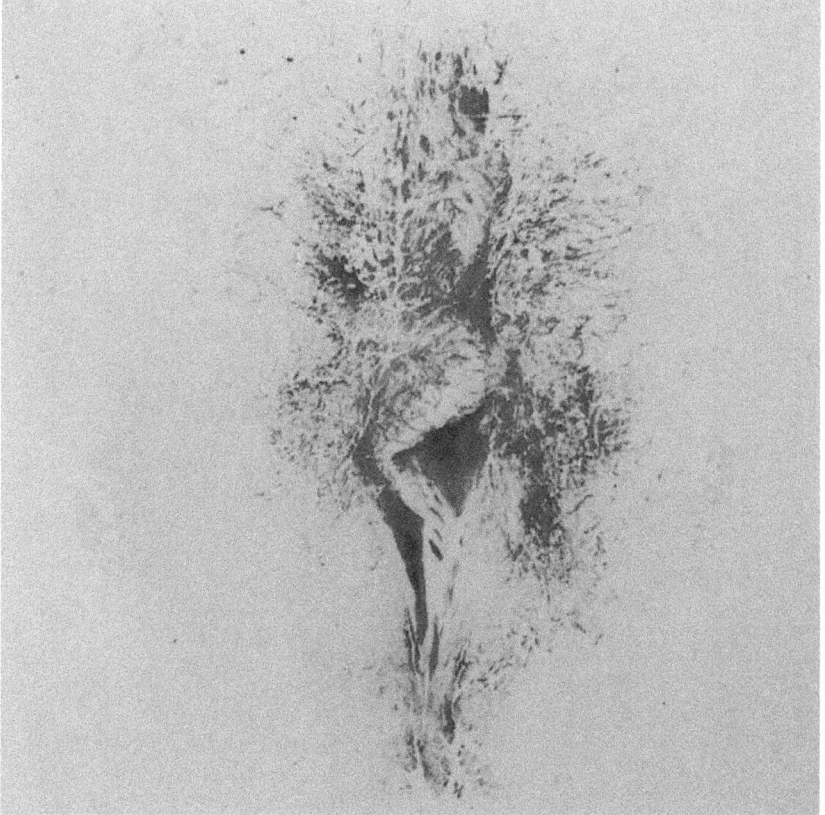

Figure 1. Pussy Print by Betty Grumble.